Cotswold D⋯

Love is in the air at Clearbrook Medical Practice!

Welcome to the idyllic Cotswolds village of Clearbrook, famous for its rolling fields of lavender and quaint cheesecake shop. No wonder it has attracted three new GPs to its medical practice. And with new doctors breathing new life into the sleepy surgery, sparks soon begin to fly!
The surprise meeting of Lorna and Oliver triggers the rekindling of a decades-old bond, while single parents and new neighbors Bella and Max are drawn to each other from the moment they meet. But when crisis threatens, are any of them brave enough to take a chance on true love?

Find out in...

Lorna and Oliver's story
Best Friend to Husband?

Bella and Max's story
Finding a Family Next Door

Both available now

Dear Reader,

I can't imagine having to start a new relationship in my fifties. Navigating a new way into a relationship, knowing how stuck in my ways I already am, LOL! So writing about a couple my age was extremely interesting, as I tried to imagine what reservations I might hold in their situation. Lorna and Oliver have a shared past, so I also pictured starting again with the boyfriend I had when I was in my late teens and it was so stressful. I'm amazed I didn't put Lorna and Oliver into therapy to deal with it all!

I hope you enjoy reading their story. I so wanted to give them their happy ending a lot quicker, but that's not how books work, so I tortured them a little before giving them their happy-ever-after and I hope you love the journey I sent them on.

Happy reading!

Louisa xxx

BEST FRIEND TO HUSBAND?

LOUISA HEATON

MEDICAL ROMANCE

Harlequin®
MEDICAL ROMANCE

Recycling programs
for this product may
not exist in your area.

ISBN-13: 978-1-335-94286-9

Best Friend to Husband?

Harlequin Enterprises ULC
22 Adelaide St. West, 41st Floor
Toronto, Ontario M5H 4E3, Canada
www.Harlequin.com

Printed in U.S.A.

Louisa Heaton lives on Hayling Island, Hampshire, with her husband, four children and a small zoo. She has worked in various roles in the health industry—most recently four years as a community first responder, answering emergency calls. When not writing, Louisa enjoys other creative pursuits, including reading, quilting and patchwork—usually instead of the things she *ought* to be doing!

Books by Louisa Heaton

Harlequin Medical Romance

Christmas North and South

A Mistletoe Marriage Reunion

Yorkshire Village Vets

Bound by Their Pregnancy Surprise

Greenbeck Village GPs

The Brooding Doc and the Single Mom
Second Chance for the Village Nurse

Night Shift in Barcelona

Their Marriage Worth Fighting For

Miracle Twins for the Midwife
Snowed In with the Children's Doctor
Single Mom's Alaskan Adventure
Finding Forever with the Firefighter
Resisting the Single Dad Surgeon

Visit the Author Profile page
at Harlequin.com for more titles.

To Nick, my Best Friend and Husband x

CHAPTER ONE

THE AIR WAS filled with the scent of lavender from the fields that surrounded the village of Clearbrook, as Dr Lorna Hudson arrived at work. It was something she loved about the village, as the soft scent filled the air. The calming aroma was normally so good before she started her day at Clearbrook Medical Practice. She used to walk in, as her cottage was only about a mile away on the edge of the village, but now she ran or jogged, as she was training for a marathon and any chance she got, she'd use. Unless she was on house calls and then she would drive in, in case she needed her vehicle that day.

But today, she'd jogged. She'd needed to burn off her anxiety, her nerves, about one of the new doctors starting today.

Dr Oliver Clandon.

Olly.

Dearest Olly. He'd been her everything during her time at medical school. Her rock. Her shoulder to cry on and, yes, she could admit, she'd had the teensiest, tiniest crush on him. A crush that had remained unrequited, because he'd been going out with Jo. And when medical school had ended, they'd both gone their separate ways, promising to keep in touch, but somehow never managing to. She'd put it down to the fact that she'd been so busy, settling into her placement as a junior doctor and beginning her GP training and, besides, she'd then been swept off her feet by Craig. It had seemed wrong to keep in touch with an old crush when she was planning a wedding and so she hadn't.

Wow. So many years have come and gone and now he's coming back.

'Did Oliver say anything in the interview about his family?' Lorna casually asked the practice manager, Priti, as she got changed out of her running gear in the staffroom and put on her work clothes. She'd been invited to Olly and Jo's wedding, which had been a surprise after they'd lost contact. The couple probably had kids by now. Grown-up kids, maybe having babies of their own.

Could Olly be a grandfather?

She felt an ache in her womb at the thought of it. A sense of unfairness and injustice. But it passed quickly. If he was a grandfather, she had no doubt, knowing the kind of man that he was, he would be an amazing one and those grand-kids would be lucky to have him.

'I can't remember him mentioning anything specific. He just said he was looking for a fresh start somewhere new, away from the hustle and bustle of an inner-city practice. Peppermint tea, or normal?' Priti waggled a box of mint tea in front of her.

'Normal's fine.' That could mean anything—a fresh start. A fresh start for him and Jo?

She hadn't been able to attend the wedding; it had fallen right in the middle of a holiday to the Maldives with Craig. With regret, she had sent back an RSVP card politely declining the invitation. She'd only met Jo briefly on occasion. Not properly. She'd tended to avoid her back then, knowing that meeting her would make her feel uncomfortable. But she had seen her once, had watched her picking up Oliver from the hospital in her car and she'd been stunningly beautiful. Hauntingly so. Long, blonde hair, the type of face that ought to be fronting an international make-up campaign or skincare regime. But dark shadows beneath her eyes.

Lorna had felt ugly compared to Jo. She'd not yet fully understood how best to use hair product to tame her ginger waves. She was self-conscious about her teeth when she smiled—even though there was nothing obviously wrong with them, she felt they were slightly crooked. It had made her crush on Oliver even more painful, knowing it would always be unrequited—when he could bag women like Jo, why would he ever look her way?

'When do they all get here?' Lorna asked, feeling her nerves set slightly on edge. The lavender scent had abated inside the building and its calming effects were long gone.

'I said nine o'clock, but their clinics don't start until ten. I thought it would give them all time to get settled in, meet you, get their rooms sorted to their preferences…'

Lorna nodded, accepting her mug of tea from Priti. 'Thanks. It's strange, isn't it? With everyone gone?'

Clearbrook Medical Practice had always been a four-doctor practice, but in the last six months, there'd been some changes. Dr Mossman had retired after thirty years' service and was currently enjoying the pleasures of a world cruise with his wife. Dr Bleaker had gone on maternity leave and had recently given birth to her first baby. And Dr O'Riordan had left to work with Doctors Without Borders. He was apparently somewhere in the Gambia.

The changes had necessitated Priti having to interview to fill the posts. Oliver had gained one place and the other two posts were going to be filled by a Dr Bella Nightingale and a Dr Max Moore, who were going to renting cottages across from one another. Oliver, Priti told her, had secured a place to rent in the centre of the village.

'Just a bit. But we can build another close-knit practice with Oliver, Max and Bella. I really liked them all in their interviews and think they'll fit in with the community. How long has it been since you saw Dr Clandon?' Priti wanted to know.

'Oh, God, years! I dread to think how many. Certainly before I got all these laughter lines and crow's feet!' Lorna joked.

Their conversation was interrupted by the reception supervisor, Saskia, popping her head around the door. 'Dr Clandon has arrived.'

Lorna felt herself tense. She couldn't understand why she was so nervous. She and Oliver had been very good friends and study partners for five long years. There was no need to feel this anxious. They'd no doubt get along like a house on fire and carry on as if they'd not been apart for decades. She glanced at herself in the mirror. The redness in her cheeks from running had gone down now. She was back to being pale and heavily freckled. She straightened her hair subconsciously, smoothed her blouse and skirt and prepared to meet an old friend.

* * *

Was it strange to feel as if he were coming home to family? Even though he'd never been to this place? Had only just moved into his cottage and his life was still in boxes? That he was about to start a new job?

She's there. In that building. Lorna.

He'd not known that she worked here when he'd first applied for the position, but when he'd begun his research into the practice before his video interview and he'd seen her photo under the staff page, his heart had begun to pound. He'd known then that out of the six places he'd applied for, this job, the one here at Clearbrook Medical Practice, was the one that he absolutely had to get.

He needed a friend—or at least a friendly face. Quite frankly, it had almost seemed to be a sign.

Oliver had arrived in the village on Saturday and had spent Sunday jogging about the village to get to know it. Running was a new thing he'd taken up recently on his travels. He didn't do it often, but he liked the way he felt afterwards. As though he'd done something good for himself. It blew away the cobwebs. After the long drive to his new place and the hours of unpacking boxes, going up and down stairs, he'd needed some fresh air. A part of him had hoped that he would somehow stumble upon Lorna in the village, but just because she worked here, didn't mean she actually *lived* here.

He knew she'd got married years ago. She'd sent him an invite, but he'd not been able to go. Jo had been having radiotherapy at the time and hadn't been feeling good. Though she'd told him to go to the wedding on his own, he'd felt bad about leaving her alone in the house. And Lorna hadn't made it to his wedding either, so did it really matter? Even though he would have loved to have seen her. She must have looked beautiful in her dress. Her hair done, her make-up done. He would have liked to have seen her like that.

He tried to picture Lorna with kids. Maybe even grandchildren. Lorna? A grandmother? He couldn't picture it. Didn't want to picture it, because then, wouldn't it mean that they were both old? That half their lives had passed by?

He couldn't wait to see her. Say hello. See that smile of hers. So wide. So bright. She used to say she hated her smile. Thought it showed too many teeth, but he'd always disagreed. She'd had a lovely smile and he wanted to see it again, to pull her into a hug and hold her for a moment. Lorna represented a happy part of his past.

If all he got to do with her each day was hug her, then that would be enough. It would have to be. Surely her husband wouldn't like it if he tried anything else.

Not that he was looking for anything more with Lorna than friendship and a good working relationship. She was married, and as for him? He had far too much baggage, and he was determined now to be a bachelor. To enjoy what he never could before: living a life of freedom, with just himself calling the shots. His years spent travelling had shown him how much he enjoyed doing that.

He walked up to the lady at Reception. A bright young thing in the practice's uniform of a royal-blue blouse and black skirt. 'Good morning. I'm Dr Clandon, the new GP.'

'Hello! I'm Saskia, the reception supervisor. Take a seat and I'll go and fetch Priti.'

He sat down in Reception and placed his briefcase on the floor beside him. It seemed to be a standard waiting room. Lines of empty chairs, walls covered in health information, reception desk off to one side. Behind the desk, he saw a board of names and there was Lorna's, right at the top. He smiled and wondered if she knew he was coming. She had to, right? How was she feeling about it? Was she excited to see him?

She'd no doubt notice a few changes. Nearly three decades had passed since they'd last seen each other. He had a bit more grey in his hair. He wore glasses now. *Nerd glasses*, his nieces reliably informed him, and he was rather proud of his short beard and moustache, even if they were also peppered with grey. He thought it made him look quite distinguished. And though he might no longer have the flat, washboard abs he'd once had as a young man, he kept himself reasonably trim and fit.

How would Lorna look?

It didn't take him long to find out.

As Priti emerged from a door down the corridor, Lorna stepped into view behind her. A broad smile crept across his face at the sight of her.

She looked lovely. As she always had. Her auburn hair was still long and fell in soft, smooth waves past her shoulders. Her blue eyes were as kind as ever and her smile…that broad smile of hers hadn't changed one jot. Once he'd shaken hands with Priti, he looked at his old best friend. 'Lorna! Good to see you after all this time!'

'You too.'

God, it was good to hear her voice. He proffered his arms for a hug and she stepped into them and, just as he'd wanted, he got his hug. He could hardly believe they were back together again. Could he keep on holding tight to her? He felt as though he had thirty years of hugs to catch up on.

She smelt like flowers and some of those sharp

edges she'd once had seemed to have softened. Before, in the early days when he'd give her a hug, she'd almost freeze. Stiffen. She wouldn't relax. But now?

He wanted to just stand there and hold her tight and tell her that he'd missed her, but he felt her pull back to take a good, long look at him. Reluctantly, he let go.

'Well, we've a lot to get through, Oliver, so if you'd like to come with me, I can give you your welcome pack,' Priti suggested.

He wished he could have a moment longer with Lorna. But he was here for a different reason. To *work*. 'Of course. I'll see you later?' he asked Lorna.

'Absolutely. Good to have you here, Olly.' She looked as though she meant it and he was glad. And she'd called him Olly, the way she used to. What was that sing-song name she'd once given him? *Olly-Wally?* Something like that, because he'd used to joke around so much in the early weeks of medical school?

Well, he was different now. He didn't joke around so much. Life had knocked him about quite a bit and though the bruises were gone, they could still hurt.

But being here with Lorna would make him feel better.

She already had.

* * *

She watched him walk away with Priti, her gaze focused on how Oliver looked.

My God, the years have been kind to him!

How was it possible that he looked so good? Maturity and years had given Olly a touch of class that she just couldn't pinpoint. Was it the fine suit? Dark grey with a hint of a checked pattern? The perfectly white shirt that was open at the neck? The highly polished shoes? Or was it those glasses? He'd never worn glasses before and they added a sense of distinction that she'd not expected. Maybe it was the beard? Peppered with silver? He'd always been clean-shaven before. Or perhaps it was the laughter lines around his eyes? Those eyes that saw right into her soul. Eyes that had always seen her for who she was: a nervous and naïve young girl who'd been so afraid of stepping out alone into the big, wide world. But someone who wanted to make a difference. To change people's lives.

Or maybe it was simply seeing his smile all over again, after all this time? It had made her feel an intensity that she'd forgotten about—the way Oliver would make her feel, just by being in his presence. It was like seeing him for the first time all over again. Oliver had been young, fresh-faced, almost cheeky-looking, with his floppy hair and natural charm. Everyone had seemed to know him and be his friend. He had been a popular, well-liked guy, and he'd seemed to have an easy confidence around people. A confidence that, she'd noted in some of their early lectures, would *disappear* as he struggled to follow some piece of chemistry or brain function. And then, in one lecture, he'd settled into a seat next to her and she'd felt so incredibly aware of him, but had been too frightened to say anything. She'd sat there, chewing on her pen and then...

Lorna turned with reluctance and headed into her consulting room where she began to boot up the computer and get ready for her clinic. As she sat down at her desk, she glanced over at the picture that had always sat there. Graduation day. The moment when everyone had thrown their caps into the air. She'd stood next to Oliver and though everyone else was looking up with joy, she and Oliver had been caught looking at each other, joy on their faces. Him, thankful for all the help she'd given him—and not just academically. All the extra study hours in the library they'd spent together, long into the early hours. The many hours they'd sat together talking about Jo. Her, already trying to hide the pain that she knew was coming when they'd go their separate ways, hoping he'd keep his promise to write or email. Wondering if that moment would be the last she'd see of him.

Lorna swallowed and looked away, bringing up her clinic listing. She had six patients this morning and the first was to check out a lump a patient had found in her breast. Verity James. She grimaced. She liked Verity. She owned the cheesecake shop in the village. A good woman. Kind.

Lorna called her in and Verity sat opposite her, looking nervous. Apprehensive. 'Verity! Hello. Take a seat. How can I help you today?'

'I found a lump when I was in the shower. Here, on this side of my breast.' She indicated the left side of her left breast.

'Okay. Does it hurt at all?'

'No.'

'You've not banged yourself, or had an injury to that side?'

'No.'

'And you've not had a cold or an infection recently, or felt unwell?'

'I've been tired and I think I'm losing weight, but I've not been trying to. I'm eating the same.'

'Busy at work?' Verity's shop was world-famous for the lavender-infused cheesecake that sold all over the globe. She'd even made cheesecakes for movie stars and royalty. The kitchen was going twenty-four hours a day, six days a week to accommodate all the online orders that they had to meet.

'It's always busy at work, but no more than usual.'

'And how long would you say you've been feeling tired?'

'I'm not sure. It kind of came on gradually, but a good six weeks or so.'

'And how much weight would you say you've lost?'

'Half a stone? I'm not sure.'

Lorna looked at Verity's last recorded weight. 'Let's get you to stand on these scales for me.' She stood up and escorted Verity over to the weighing scales in the corner of the room. 'Hmm. You've lost more than half a stone, Vee. It's more like fifteen pounds.'

'I didn't realise it was that much.'

'Any fevers? Night sweats?'

'One or two, but isn't that just menopause?'

'Maybe. But it might be worth doing some bloodwork, too. Let me just take your temperature.' Verity's temperature was normal on examination. 'And if you'd like to go behind the curtain, I'll perform a breast examination, if that's all right? I'll just be one moment to fetch a chaperone.' Lorna left the room to look for the nurse or HCA that worked at the clinic and managed to grab hold of Carrie, in between taking bloods.

'You know Carrie?' Lorna called as she re-entered the room.

'Of course,' Verity said from behind the curtain. 'Ready.'

Lorna put on gloves and she and Carrie went behind the curtain. 'We'll examine both breasts and I'll look at the right breast first, okay?'

'Yes.'

Lorna performed a visual examination first, looking for puckering, discolouration or another sign that might indicate something going on with the breast. She checked the nipples, too, looking for inversion, but everything seemed normal. 'Lie down for me.'

Verity lay and Lorna then performed a physical examination of Verity's breasts. The right one was fine, with no sign of any lumps in the breast, armpit or chest. Then she began the examination of the left breast. She felt the lump immediately and palpated it to see if it was adhered to any tissue, or if she could move it. It was small, maybe half a centimetre. 'I can feel it. We'll definitely need to get this checked out. Okay, you can get dressed for me. Thanks, Carrie.'

Carrie left the room and when Verity emerged from behind the curtain, Lorna talked her through the referral they had to do in instances such as this. 'You'll receive an appointment at the breast clinic within two weeks. You'll see a consultant, have a mammogram and an ultrasound, and should receive the results at the appointment. It's probably just a cyst, but it's best to get it checked out.' Lorna hoped the night sweats and the weight loss were incidental, but you never could be too sure with something like this. 'Any history of breast issues in the family?'

'My mother's sister had breast cancer. She ended up having a double mastectomy.'

Lorna nodded. 'Okay. It's definitely good that you've caught whatever this is early.'

'Let's hope so. Thanks, Lorna.'

'Take care, Verity.'

As she typed her notes, Lorna couldn't help but think of her own mother, whom she'd lost to breast cancer six years ago. It was a loss that should never have happened. Her mother had said nothing about her lump, thinking it would go away, and had been too scared to ask her daughter about it. She'd figured that, as there was no history of any other family members having breast cancer, it couldn't possibly be anything serious, until she started to feel really unwell. By the time she'd made it into hospital, the cancer had metastasised into her brain and bones, and it had been too late to treat it.

Watching her mother die in palliative care had

been an awful thing that Lorna wouldn't wish on anybody, and it had been a huge wake-up call to her entire family. Lorna now made sure that everyone did everything that they could to maintain their health. She ensured that her father completed the routine bowel-health tests and prostate exams when they were asked for. That her brothers stopped smoking and began eating healthier and going to the gym. And Lorna? She'd started running as often as she could, and examined her own breasts every three months alongside her regular smear tests and NHS health checks.

She hoped Verity would be okay, but there was nothing they could do now but wait.

A knock on her door interrupted her thoughts. 'Come in.'

Priti opened her door. 'Just popping in so you can quickly meet Bella and Max.' Priti opened the door wide and stepped in, followed by a beautiful young woman with long dark hair and an extremely attractive young man with blond hair and a beard.

Lorna stood up and held out her hand in greeting. 'Pleased to meet you. I'm Lorna.' She shook their hands. 'Did you find us all right?'

'Yes, thanks,' said Bella, nodding.

'It was easy enough. Thankfully the clinic is near the infant school,' said Max, smiling.

'Oh, that's right. Priti said you'd both got young kids. How old?'

'Ewan's four.'

Max nodded. 'Rosie, too.'

'Same age? Maybe they'll be best friends, then? Well, welcome to Clearbrook. It's good to have you both with us. Maybe I'll get to catch up with you both later on.'

'Looking forward to it,' said Bella.

Lorna's computer beeped to let her know her next patient had arrived in Reception. 'We'll let you get on,' said Priti. 'I'll show you to your rooms.' She ushered Max and Bella out of Lorna's consulting room, and Lorna sat back down at the computer to finish her notes on Verity and make the referral.

Bella and Max seemed lovely. She was looking forward to getting to know them both better. They'd had such a lovely clinic when Clive, Tilly and Ben, the outgoing three doctors, had been here. They'd been like a small family. She had been sad to see them all go. Had even begun to question if she herself ought to move on. She'd been here at Clearbrook for eight long years, after all.

But she was happy here. Settled. She loved living in Clearbrook and couldn't imagine ever being anywhere else. And when Priti had offered her the senior partnership, she'd accepted the post gladly.

The next patient to enter her consulting room was Michael Cooper. The only note accompanying his appointment was stomach pain, so she called him through.

Michael came into her room, looking uncomfortable, one hand on his abdomen, as he slowly lowered himself into the chair.

'Morning, Michael. It says here you've got a bit of tummy pain—why don't you tell me about that?'

'It started this morning about two a.m. I'd got up for a wee and felt fine, to be honest, but just as I was flushing the loo, I got hit by these sudden stomach pains. I could barely stand. I think I crawled back to my bed somehow. Took some paracetamol, which helped a little, but my stomach hurts so much!'

'Can you show me where the pain is?'

He rubbed the area above his belly button, but below his ribcage. 'I'm sorry to hear that. How would you rate that pain on a scale of one to ten, with one being barely anything at all and ten being the worst?'

'About a seven. Maybe a six or a five once the painkiller kicks in.'

She took his blood pressure, checked his SATs

and his temperature, which were all normal. 'Any nausea, vomiting or diarrhoea?'

'I feel a little bit sick, but I haven't actually been sick.'

'And yesterday, you didn't have a fall, or bang into anything, or lift anything too heavy?'

'No.' Michael shook his head.

'Did you eat or drink anything different yesterday?'

Michael nodded. 'I did, yeah. I had a couple of pints down at the pub. I don't normally drink, but my nephew was here visiting. He's come over from Ireland and he kind of encouraged me to have a pint or two.'

'And how would you describe the pain? Is it burning pain? Stabbing? Aching?'

'It just hurts, Doctor. I'm not sure I could describe it.'

'Let's examine you.' She encouraged Michael to get up onto her examination couch, so she could palpate his abdomen. It was soft and he didn't react or show pain when she pressed down. It didn't make him feel worse with her poking and prodding him. 'You can get up now. I think you've probably got a touch of gastritis. That means your stomach is inflamed and irritated. That's causing the pain and the slight nausea you feel. I'm going to write you a prescription for some omeprazole to protect your stomach and some codeine for the pain, okay? I want you to take them regularly for at least a week and if you're still in pain after that, give us another call. Okay?'

'Will do, Doc. Thanks.'

'In the meantime, no more alcohol, no spicy foods. Try and eat simply until this passes.'

'Yes, thanks.' Michael took the prescription and left her room.

Lorna quickly typed her notes, then realised she'd had a couple of blood reports and hospital letters appear in her inbox for previous patients. She checked those, noting further treatments, and got the ladies on Reception to call those that she needed to see again. After that, she worked her way through the rest of her patient list until morning break. She headed off to the staffroom to make herself a quick cup of tea and to grab an apple from her lunchbox.

Max, one of the new doctors, was in there, having just made himself a drink.

'Hey. How's it going? Finding everything all right?' Lorna asked him.

'Yes, thanks. I am. How's your morning going?'

'Not bad at all.'

'I got a chance to speak to Dr Clandon. Oliver. He tells me that you two knew each other way back.'

She smiled and nodded. 'Medical school. Yeah.'

'Must be weird meeting up with each other after all this time. I bet you've got a lot to talk about.'

'I'm sure there are a few stories we could tell each other.' She thought of all that Oliver had missed. Things she wished she could have told him about when they'd happened, but she'd never maintained contact. It had felt wrong to, especially as they had both been with partners, getting on with their lives. Her name was different on her social media profiles to protect her identity from patients. A lot of doctors did it, so if Oliver had tried to contact her, he would have had difficulty. She could have told him about her mum. Her relationship with Craig. The fertility treatments. Then Craig's betrayal. Feeling as though she had lost everything and having to start anew, all alone.

But Lorna didn't normally like to focus on the bad things in life. She tried to always press forward. To be optimistic. What was the point in wallowing? Maybe she'd tell Oliver about these things and maybe she wouldn't. And even if he did find out, what could he do about it? It was in the past and he'd made a life with Jo now.

Briefly, she wondered what Jo was going to do in the village. Did she have a job? Was she going to commute elsewhere? She'd not thought to ask him this morning how his wife was.

I must remember to do that.

Jo had been through a lot. That early cancer scare during medical school had really thrown Olly. His partner going through chemo when she was still only a young woman on the brink of living her life must have made them both re-evaluate what was important.

'Have you managed to get everything unpacked yet, or are you still living out of boxes?'

Max laughed. 'I'd love to tell you that I'm perfectly organised and everything's done, but unfortunately, no. There's still a lot to do, but I unpacked the important bits and my daughter's room is done.'

'Rosie, right?'

'Yes.'

'How old is she again?'

'Four.' He smiled. 'Let me show you a picture.' Max got out his mobile phone and Lorna dutifully looked and made all the right noises.

Rosie was indeed a lovely-looking young girl. Same hair colour as her father, but that was where the resemblance ended. 'She doesn't look like you. Does she take after her mum?'

Max's eyes darkened slightly. 'Yes. She does.'

Lorna wasn't sure if she'd said something out of line, but something about Max had changed.

She hoped she'd not upset him, by asking about Rosie's mother. She wanted to make the conversation return to its brighter overall tone. 'And she's going to the local infant school here in Clearbrook?'

Max nodded, putting away his phone into his back pocket.

'I've heard it's very good. One of the teachers there is a patient of mine. Miss Celic?'

'Yes, that's Rosie's teacher.'

'Oh, she'll have a wonderful time with her. Everyone rates her.'

'That's good to know.'

Lorna began to make herself a cup of tea and it was at that moment that Oliver walked into the staffroom. He looked from Max to Lorna and said hello.

'Looks like we're all on the same mission,' he said, grabbing a mug from the cupboard and dropping a teabag into it.

It was weird having him so close. Since the hug this morning, she'd tried to keep her mind off how it had felt to be pressed up against him. But his physical presence was having a weird effect on her. She could see his arm muscles through his shirt. He had nicely defined biceps that made her think of strength and safety. That he could be the type of man to protect you if you needed. She liked that, but tried not to stare. 'Tea is essential,' she said.

'Absolutely.' Max's phone began to ring and he pulled it from his pocket and glanced at the screen. 'Excuse me.' And he left the room.

Lorna became acutely aware that she and Oliver were alone together for the first time since meeting again. She'd thought it would be the same. Two friends who would just slip back into exactly how it was before.

Only it wasn't like that at all. She felt incredibly aware of him. 'How's Jo?' she asked, unable to think of anything to say, but feeling the need to cut the tension in the air.

He shrugged. Tried to look nonchalant. 'Fine. I think.'

Lorna frowned, puzzled. 'You think? You don't know?'

'Not really. I haven't seen her for years.'

Years? Lorna swallowed. 'What happened?'

'We got a divorce.'

'Oh.'

She almost couldn't believe it! Jo and Olly *divorced*? The way they'd been together before, she'd thought they were a for-ever couple. He'd seemed so dedicated to her. They'd been through so much! The worst that life could throw at them—a difficult, long-term, life-threatening illness—so what had been the thing that broke them apart? Was he single, then?

No. Not possible. Not looking like that. There has to be someone else.

The second his divorce papers had come through, there'd been a part of Oliver that had wanted to rush off and track Lorna down. Find her. Spend time with her, rekindle a friendship that he'd never been able to achieve with anyone else. Lorna had understood him completely. Probably because he'd been able to be himself with her and known he wouldn't get judged. Because he'd known he could talk to her about his fears and she wouldn't call him out for being weak. When he spoke to his male friends and the talks got serious, they had a tendency to laugh things off. Make a joke of them. Lorna hadn't. She'd sat quietly and listened. He'd felt *seen*.

So much of his relationship with Jo had been all about *her*, and rightly so, but sometimes he'd needed someone to check on him. That was what Lorna had done. In those formative years, the two of them had got on like a house on fire. Lorna had helped get him through medical school, when all his mind had been able to focus on was caring for someone with cancer, alongside chemo drugs and their side effects. Nausea. Exhaustion.

Without Lorna, he would have failed his exams. He'd somehow got into medical school by the skin of his teeth and right away he had begun to struggle with the level of work, the assessments, the studying, the revising, the tests—but somehow, she had calmed him down. Got him to focus. Turned him from the joker he'd once been into a serious student who knew how to revise properly. Who made his own set of flashcards.

She'd somehow known what to dangle in front of him, like a donkey following a carrot on a stick. She'd bought tickets to a comedy show after they'd passed their first OSCE assessment. OSCEs were the Objective Structured Clinical Examinations, which demonstrated that a student could carry out clinical skills such as history-taking, physical exams, blood draws, medical knowledge and order writing. She'd bought a ticket for Jo, too, but Jo hadn't gone. She'd been too ill.

At the end of their first-year exams, she'd booked them in to complete a Colour Run around a local park, completing a five-kilometre race over a series of obstacles whilst having coloured powder thrown over them by supporters. He'd taken her to see a film as a thank you after their first successful placements. They'd gone with three others to Brighton for a pride parade.

And all the time, no matter where they'd been, she had quizzed him on his medical knowledge. He'd present her with case scenarios for her to diagnose in return. It had become a game. One Lorna had seemed to enjoy playing. In short, she had supported him when everyone else in his family had expected him to fail. And she'd been there, long into the night, when he'd called her needing to talk to someone about Jo's cancer battle. Researching with him at all hours, to find him the information he needed to sit in the room with those oncologists and advocate for his girlfriend.

And he'd always felt, despite trying, that he could never give her enough back.

Oliver had met Jo at college, doing A levels. She'd been in his science classes, because Jo had wanted to become a veterinary surgeon. She'd been gorgeous. Funny. Witty. Full of life. They'd had great fun together and started to go out seriously. They'd each applied to neighbouring universities and got in, celebrating with a weekend trip to Paris. It was there that he'd thought he could feel a lump in her breast.

Jo had dismissed it at first, even though she'd told him she would get it checked out, and for months during their first year at uni she'd told him it had been checked out and it was nothing. Only she hadn't. She'd lied to him, because she had actually been very afraid. One day her lies had caught up with her and he'd discovered the truth, so he'd made her an appointment and gone with her to the GP, sitting in the waiting room and praying that it was just a cyst.

It hadn't been, and that was the day their lives had changed. And changed again weeks later when they'd discovered that the cancer was already Stage Three. He'd felt so angry because if she'd just gone when they'd first discovered the lump, maybe things wouldn't have ended up the way they did.

He'd felt bad about being angry with her. She'd had cancer. How could he have been angry? Their relationship had been on unsteady waters for a while after that. He'd stayed by her side, though, because Lorna had helped him process that anger. Made him see that he wasn't angry at Jo, but at the cancer and what it had been taking from them both.

It had taken from Lorna, too. Because he ought to have been a better friend to her, paid her more attention, found out about what was going off in her life, rather than just focusing on his own and yet, selflessly, she had always been there for him. He'd wondered, once, if she'd liked him as more than a friend. But she'd never said anything. Never made any move, which had probably been for the best, because he would have had to turn her down and that might have ruined their friendship, which he'd valued so much.

Lorna had lamented that in all the time she'd been at medical school, she'd not met one guy whom she'd thought she could be with and that she'd end up a lonely spinster surrounded by cats. And he'd tried to help. Had tried to set her up with various guys, whom she'd go out with for one date and then never see again.

He'd be lying if he denied often thinking about whether life with Lorna would have been better, but what was the point in that? He couldn't have walked out on Jo. Not whilst she'd been going through the battle for her life. What would that have said about him? He wasn't heartless. But he'd been able to feel Lorna slipping away. Medical school had been at an end, they'd both got jobs in different hospitals, they hadn't been going to see each other every day any more. Lorna wouldn't be there and he would miss his best friend in the whole wide world. And she'd told him, right at the end, that she wished things had been different for them, before she'd stepped on a train and out of his life...

A statement that had made him question everything.

But he had not stayed in touch with Lorna. He knew why. He'd wanted to. He'd promised to. But he'd been trying to make things work with Jo. She'd needed him and he'd known that if he'd kept in touch with Lorna, it would have felt, somehow, as if he were cheating on Jo. Even though he and Lorna had only ever been friends.

He was an honourable guy.

He'd done it for his marriage. He'd made a choice to stay with Jo and he hadn't wanted that sacrifice to be for nothing, so he'd given his marriage one hundred per cent.

And still *failed*.

All that work, all that sacrifice, had been for nothing.

Left with nothing. Nothing to show for all the sacrifices he'd made for her, except for divorce papers and no family. He'd never felt so alone. Lost. He'd thought about Lorna then. Missed her soothing words. Her friendship. Had briefly considered getting in touch with her, but had decided not to, because what would she think of him getting in touch only when he needed something? It had felt selfish. Wrong. And he'd wanted her to live her life, without him striding back into it, needing her.

And so instead of finding Lorna, he'd taken some time to discover *who* he was and what he wanted from life now. Years of taking locum posts. Travelling. Globe-trotting. Just sitting with who he was and what he wanted from life.

Having experiences. He'd come back knowing he wanted peace. Quiet. He wanted to live somewhere beautiful and so he'd done an Internet search for the most beautiful villages in England. He'd found Clearbrook in the top ten. Then he'd done searches for GP vacancies and there it had been. Clearbrook had had vacancies. And weirdly, strangely, *miraculously*... Clearbrook had Lorna.

And he'd felt as if it was meant to be.

'So, I have a question.' Oliver stood with his mug of tea, looking at Lorna. He knew that she had never thought of herself as beautiful. She felt her auburn hair was unruly and that her freckles made her stand out in the wrong way. She thought her body was nondescript, and she didn't care for fashion, but rather comfort.

But he thought she was beautiful. He always had. And in the years that had passed since they'd last seen one another, Lorna had clearly found her style. Her long, auburn hair was wavy, and cascaded around her face beautifully. Her freckles were as gorgeous as they always had been, but she wore a little make-up now that focused the gaze on her eyes and lips. She looked strong and fit and her clothes were timeless. She was wearing a summery dress in a jungle print, lots of leaves and green and somewhere in there were brightly coloured birds. She'd teamed the outfit with a nifty little pair of heeled ankle boots. And he had forgotten how great she smelled.

'Oh?' She looked at him with curiosity.

'We've not seen each other for a long time. We ought to spend some time catching up.'

Lorna smiled. 'That wasn't a question.'

He loved her smile. It made his heart glad to see it again. 'I wondered if you'd like to go out for a meal. You can bring Craig—it'll all be above board.'

Lorna's eyes darkened and she looked away. 'Craig and I are no longer together. I'm divorced, too.'

'Oh. Well, okay, you can bring whoever you're with, then.'

She blushed. 'I'm not with anyone.'

Lorna was single? His heart began to beat rapidly. He'd never expected that. Not in a million years! Craig had let her go? Was the man stupid? 'What happened?'

She smiled. 'Maybe we should talk about that over dinner? I've got to get back to my clinic.'

'Of course. Are you free tonight?'

Lorna nodded. 'I am.'

'Know any good places around here? I'm new.' He smiled and winked at her, the way he used to.

She laughed. 'Jasper's is good. Casual dining. Excellent range of food. Decent prices.'

He nodded. 'Then I'll give them a call.'

CHAPTER TWO

I'M GOING OUT to dinner with Olly.

She couldn't believe this was happening. Hearing he was going to join her practice had been one thing. She'd figured, though, that he'd be married still, and that at some point, yes, they'd probably go out for dinner with Jo, as a sort of reunion celebration. She'd psyched herself up for that.

But dinner with just the two of them?

Knowing that he was single? Same as her?

She wasn't looking for a relationship these days. She was quite happy being single. She was good at it, too. Her cottage was exactly as she liked it. Her job was wonderful. She ate out alone quite happily. She let no one down and they didn't let her down. No one said mean things. She went to the movies whenever she wanted. Did whatever she wanted. Took cruise holidays and made friends whenever the desire took her for some time away to see the world. She liked her routines. Her life. Olly being back in her life would just add to that. Having her best friend back. It would be the icing on the cake, but she didn't need any more than that and, besides, he'd never shown any romantic interest in her, anyway. She'd only ever been his friend. That was the box she resided in for him, and that was enough. Even if she had once harboured feelings for him, and even if she did still find him incredibly attractive.

It would be wrong to let it become anything else.

Why ruin a beautiful friendship?

He was never interested in me anyway and why pursue rejection? I've just got him back. He could be back for good. Why take the risk of ruining our friendship?

Lorna had put on a flowing white dress, put her hair up in clips and allowed a few tendrils to fall. She liked how her hair looked when she did it that way. It was showy, yet casual, and she wanted to look a little different from how she'd looked at work all day. Wanted to feel confident. To show Oliver that she was different from the mouse she'd been before. Some strappy sandals and a couple of ankle bracelets completed the look and once she'd spritzed herself with perfume, she was ready to go.

In the past, Olly had always been a little late, but at seven-thirty on the dot, she heard his knock at the door and the butterflies in her stomach began to flutter.

She grabbed her clutch and opened the door. 'Wow. Look at you!' she said, admiring his look. Oliver was wearing dark trousers and a pale blue shirt, open at the neck.

'Look at *you*!' he said in reply, palms outward. 'You look stunning.'

'Thanks.' She tried not to blush, but it was hard when she wanted the compliment. Wanted him to notice that she knew how to dress herself these days. Knew her style. What worked for her. When they'd been in medical school, she'd not known what clothing worked for her and so she'd often hidden beneath oversized hoodies and jumpers, teaming them with jeans or baggy cargo pants.

'Ready to go?'

'Let me just lock up.' She turned and locked her front door, dropping her keys into the small clutch she'd brought with her. When she turned, he held out his arm and she slipped her own through his. 'We're walking?'

'If that's all right? It's such a lovely night.'

'That's fine. Let's go.' They had a reservation at eight. Olly had popped into her room at work in the afternoon to tell her he'd made the reservation and she was looking forward to getting something to eat.

Lorna often ate at Jasper's, but previously she'd always dined there alone, or on occasion with Priti or Clive for a work meeting. It was going to be nice to eat there with Olly. 'This still feels a little surreal.'

Oliver smiled at her. 'Walking?'

She nudged him playfully with her elbow. He'd always been a joker. 'No! You. Being here. After all this time.'

'Glad to be here.'

'Did you know I was here, when you applied?'

'Honestly? Not at first. I sent in the application and figured I'd research the post later if I got offered an interview and when I realised you were on staff...well... I almost went running in the other direction.' He laughed.

'Olly!'

'No, seriously, when I knew you were here, it made me want this job even more.'

She smiled, hearing him say that. It felt good to know he wanted to be back with her.

'I should never have lost touch with you.'

'It happens.' She didn't want him to feel bad. 'I wasn't great at keeping in touch either. The first few years after graduation are crazy—whenever I got free time, I just wanted to sleep.'

'They were the worst, weren't they?' he agreed. 'I remember this one nightmare shift that never seemed to end. I was triaging minors in an accident and emergency department in London. Started at eight at night and I was meant to finish at eight in the morning. But we were slammed. Short-staffed. The department overrun with patients, you felt like you never made any progress. Eight a.m. came and went. Then nine. Then ten. Then I was asked if I could carry on until five p.m. to cover for someone who'd not made it in and you know what it's like. You're young. Eager. You want to impress and show you're one of the team. Jo was doing okay, so I stayed, and by the time I got home it was around seven-thirty that evening. I think I passed out for almost a whole day.' He shook his head. 'It made me realise that I had to learn to say no, for my own health and sanity. These days I don't think they let you work that long. For safety reasons.'

'I hear you. Those first two years of working as a doctor almost put me off, but I knew that if I could just get through it, then I could begin my general practitioner training and do the job that I wanted to do.'

'Strange how we both became GPs.'

'I know! I always thought that you'd want the adrenaline of being a surgeon, or something.'

'Really?'

'Yes. I remember being on placement with you

and we were both observing an appendectomy. You looked fascinated.'

'Never even made my specialism top ten.'

'Was GP training always your number one?'

He nodded. 'Actually, yes, it was. I wanted to be able to build a rapport with my patients. Know them over time. Watch them have children and then treat those children. I liked the continuity of that. I think it's because I remember growing up, when we had this family doctor who I saw all the time. Dr Spencer, his name was. Lovely guy. And I just remember how I used to feel seeing him. Knowing that he knew me. That he'd known me for a long time and how comfortable that made me feel. I wanted to make other people feel the same way about me.'

'That's nice. But you've moved here where you have to start again? Get to know a whole load of new families? That wasn't daunting? Or upsetting, having to leave the families you did know behind?'

'No. I was never able to build that kind of relationship. What with Jo and needing to be there for her, I did a lot of locum work. She did, too, when she was able, and we moved to pursue a big job she wanted. I've never felt settled in one place. Don't get me wrong, locum money is great, but I wanted that community feel, you know? I took time for myself after the divorce just travelling and finding myself and deciding on what I want to do and…yeah…here I am.'

'Here you are. And we're very glad to have you here. *I'm* glad to have you here.'

'Good.'

The village looked very pretty this evening. To be fair, it looked pretty all the time. Clearbrook had been declared an Area of Outstanding Natural Beauty. The scent of lavender from the fields filled the air. Fat bumblebees were still flitting from flower to flower, even this late in the day. Lorna saw foxgloves and hollyhocks and marigolds spilling over walls. Jasmine and clematis climbing over doorways and trellises. Everywhere was leafy and green and birds sang happily.

It was peaceful.

It was perfect.

And she was here to experience it with Oliver. She'd never have imagined that he would come here and yet here he was. Ready to put down roots, by all accounts, and that made her happy.

'Here we are. Jasper's.'

Jasper's was an old building, Grade II listed, built of local stone and adorned with hanging baskets and window boxes. There was some seating outside for people that just wanted drinks. The dining tables were inside and out the back, where they had a large garden, the tables were protected by large umbrellas. The garden over-looked the local woods and a small lake, where ducks, geese and swans would lazily glide.

'Looks great. After you.' Oliver held the door open for her and she smiled as she passed him, feeling hungry and looking forward to having something nice to eat. She told herself that this was just friends catching up. It could never be anything more, because she didn't want to be a disappointment to anyone ever again. The way she'd felt she'd been to Craig.

She was never disappointed with Jasper's, however. The food was filling, local and had ample servings that, if you didn't finish, they'd let you take home with you.

Inside, a low light, created by wall sconces and mood lighting, revealed an interior that was classic and comfortable. White linen table-cloths on round tables. A bud vase, filled with sprigs of fresh lavender, sitting in the centre of each. Wooden chairs, each painted a different soft pastel colour. Walls filled with old black and white photographs of the lavender farmers through years past. People harvesting the flow-ers. Horses pulling carts, piled high with the lav-ender in neatly tied bunches. An old market stall, complete with seller in apron and flat cap, his ancient, grizzled face lined with a history untold.

Their host for the evening was Rupert, Jasper's business partner and husband, and also one of Lorna's patients. He welcomed them warmly and escorted them to a table situated near the double doors that led outside to the garden, giving them a fabulous view of the lake and the woods beyond.

'Can I get you any drinks?' Rupert asked.

Lorna, who didn't very often drink alcohol, asked for a fresh orange with lemonade and Oliver joined her.

'This looks great,' he said. 'Look at that view! I had no idea there was a lake here in Clearbrook.'

'This used to be a bit of a manor house in years past and the owner had the lake dug out for him, so it's not actually natural. Apparently, he was into fishing and stocked the lake with fish.'

'Old money, huh? I wonder what happened to him?'

'I'm not sure, but I bet Rupert would know.'

As if summoned, Rupert arrived with their drinks on a tray.

'What happened to the guy that had the lake built here? Do you know?'

'I do! Sad story of unrequited love, I'm afraid. He was the Earl of Witton and legend has it he fell for a serving girl when this place was a manor. Their love was forbidden and the earl's mother wasn't too pleased about it, so she would harass this poor girl and make her do all this menial work to try and break her. Make her leave. But the poor lass wouldn't. She stayed. It's said that the earl's mother wanted to go out on a horse ride around the grounds and made the servant girl fetch her saddle and tack and the horse startled and kicked her in the head. The poor girl didn't survive. People think the mother was hoping something like that might happen but it was never proven. The earl remained single the rest of his life, refusing to marry and refusing to give his mother the heirs she said were his duty and after that the manor fell into disrepair.'

'That's so sad!' said Lorna. 'Imagine not being able to be with the one person who made you happy. Thank goodness we don't live in those sorts of times any more.'

'I guess it depends where you live,' Rupert said. 'Jasper and I weren't allowed to get married for a long time, remember?'

Lorna nodded. 'You two must be coming up on a big anniversary soon?'

'Ten years this autumn.'

'Ten years! Are you going to do anything special?'

'Well, if I have my way, we're going skiing, but you know what Jasper's like. He only wants to admire things from a distance and he keeps talking about this glacier express thing he's seen.'

'Well, that sounds amazing. Can't you do both?'

'Depends if you order the lobster or not, my love! Those things are expensive.' Rupert winked and left them with their menus to decide on what they wanted to eat.

'Friend or patient?' Oliver asked with a smile.

She laughed. 'Both. And neighbours. Rupert and Jasper live right next door to me.'

Oliver perused the menu with a smile. 'So, shall we pick the lobster and send them on their way to Switzerland, or nibble at a garden salad and keep them here?'

'Actually, I'm rather craving their beef wellington. I've had it before and it's marvellous. A singular taste sensation that you'll be talking about for weeks.'

Olly raised an eyebrow. 'That good, huh? Well, okay. I'll be guided by you.'

'And you have to try the local lavender cheesecake with honeycomb for dessert. Or the raspberry and rose ice cream. Or the profiteroles! Oh! Choose anything! It's all good!' She laughed.

Oliver smiled at her. 'You haven't changed at all.'

She looked flustered then. 'How do you mean?'

'Before, whenever we'd go out to eat anywhere, you would love everything. Caramel popcorn at the cinema. Or hot dogs with all the trimmings. Then there was that kebab place we'd go to after the pub and you could never make up your mind what sort of kebab you wanted, because you liked them all and the owner, Christos, would make you a little mash-up of everything.'

Lorna gasped. 'Oh, I'd forgotten about Christos! Oh, he was a lovely guy, wasn't he? I wonder what he's doing now.'

'Well, he was in his sixties back then, so he's either very old, or...'

Oliver didn't need to finish his sentence. She knew what he meant. It made her feel a little sad. 'Well, I'm going to hope that he's still with us somewhere. He did have that ancient grandmother—perhaps they're all long-lived in his family and he's sitting somewhere right now eating a chicken souvlaki. To Christos.' She raised her glass.

Oliver clinked her glass with his own. 'To Christos and his marvellous tzatziki that has never been beaten.'

They sipped their drinks and laughed. It felt good to reminisce. Felt even better to be sitting across a table from Oliver again.

How many times had they done this? Over meals? Over revision books? Flashcards? At a pub? A library? He might have needed her booksmarts at university, but she, in turn, had needed him and he'd helped her for the better. She'd been a mouse to begin with. The quiet one in the corner, who no one had wanted to hang out with. When she'd tried to make friends, she'd struggled, feeling as though she'd never quite fitted in, or had a voice loud enough to be heard over everyone else. And then one day, Oliver had simply slid into a seat next to her and struck up a conversation.

She could remember the shock she'd felt at being noticed by the most handsome guy in the room, feeling nervous at having him so close, but when she'd discovered that he had a girl-friend and that it wasn't some trick, or dare by his friends, she had begun to relax. Becoming study partners had helped her revise, too. She'd admired his easy way of being in the world. His carefree nature. His laughter. His smile. He'd been warmth, when she'd felt cold. Softness, when she'd felt sharp. A welcome when she'd felt alone. And because she'd been in Oliver's orbit, she'd got to know his friends too and they'd be-come her friends. As she'd opened up and felt more comfortable, medical school had become a lot easier, fun as well as educational, and she'd loved every minute of it. The early starts, the cadaver practice, the tests, the assessments, be-cause throughout it all, Oliver had stayed by her side.

She'd missed him when they'd gone their

separate ways. Had felt all alone again as she'd headed out into the harsh real world, without his reassuring presence at her side. Had needed his heart-warming presence when she'd gone through the worst upset of her life.

And now he was here. After all this time. Sitting opposite. Smiling at her.

Why had they ever lost touch?

Why had she allowed that to happen?

She wanted to tell him that she'd missed him. She wanted to tell him that life had not been the same without him. But she knew she couldn't do that. She was too afraid.

As Rupert arrived at their table with a smile and their beef wellingtons, she waited for him to go, then looked at Oliver over the table. 'So... should we catch up?'

'Why not? We've kinda been circling each other all night.'

'Is Jo...okay? After the whole cancer thing?'

He nodded. 'As far as I'm aware she is. We don't really talk now since the divorce, but yeah, she's in remission and has been for years.'

'That's good.' She meant it. 'I'm glad. I know you two went through a lot together. I don't know how you managed to get through medical school with all of that going on.'

'She had it harder than me. And besides, I had you.'

It meant a lot to hear him say that. That she'd been worthwhile. Of value. 'And she had *you*. So what happened between you two?'

Oliver let out a big sigh. 'What didn't happen between us?' he asked. 'The cancer thing went on for quite a few years. Chemo, radiation, surgery, recovery. Remission. Recurrence. More chemo. When she finally got the all-clear, we were *so happy*. I remember thinking, *Now. Now is the time for us to live.* To live a life that wasn't centred around the hospital and the oncology ward, you know? It was strange, I don't mind admitting. Jo was struggling to accept that for now she was free of it. Every twinge, every pain, every headache, she would worry, but her scans kept coming back clear and we began to think about the next stage of our marriage.'

'Children?'

He nodded. 'Jo had frozen her eggs before treatment all those years ago and so we knew that if we were going to have kids, it would be through IVF. So we started monitoring Jo's body a different way. Temperatures. Blood tests. Scans. Injections. Hormones. It was like we'd swapped one regime for another and it was all we could talk about. It hit us hard. It hit me hard, seeing her go through all of that and each time an implantation failed, I wanted us to wait awhile before we tried again. To recover. Maybe just have some time for us? Maybe go travelling, see the world, enjoy life, before we went into another round.

'It caused arguments because Jo just wanted to try and try again. She felt like she'd already waited far too long and she began to feel that maybe I didn't want a baby as much as she wanted one and, honestly? At one point, I didn't. I didn't think it was worth it, all the stress, all the mood swings, all the upset and the grief each time her period arrived or the test read negative. I was trying to give her a break. I was trying to let her see that there was more to life than what we had and we began to drift apart.

'When the third cycle failed, I said no more. It hurt me too, but she couldn't see that at all. She thought I wasn't affected, but she was wrong. So wrong! I would have *loved* to have a kid, but it wasn't happening and I didn't want to keep going through that heartbreak when we could have just lived instead and enjoyed each other, the way we'd never been able to before.'

He looked down at his plate. Lorna could see that he was hurt and all she wanted to do was reach out and comfort him, as she always had. But events in her own past relationship stopped her. Craig had made her doubt herself. Had told her that she wasn't enough for him and she'd begun to question if she would ever be enough for anyone. 'I'm so sorry.'

He shook his head. 'The IVF didn't work for us and, in her anger, she blamed me for it all and we couldn't come back from that, so we got divorced, years ago.'

Lorna felt nothing but sorrow for what he had been through. 'I wish I could have been there to hold your hand through all of that.'

He sighed. 'Yeah. Me too. But I'm not sure Jo would have liked that.'

'Why?'

'Because I spent all of my time with you at med school and because you never went out of your way to spend time with her, she felt that, well…she was being avoided for a reason. That you had feelings for me.'

'What?' Lorna feigned even more shock, to show that she was appalled at such a suggestion, surprised at it, but deep down, she knew the truth. Yes, Oliver had been her best friend and study partner, but she *had* harboured deeper feelings for him. Feelings that she could never have expressed because he had been with Jo and Lorna was not ever going to be the other woman. She did not want to be part of some sordid affair, or break up a couple. She'd always wanted one hundred per cent of a guy's feelings, not what he could spare for her when his girlfriend or wife wasn't around. 'But we were just friends,' she protested. 'Study buddies. You told her that, right?'

'Of course I did!' Oliver shook his head and smiled before sipping his drink, as if Jo's suggestion had been the most ridiculous thing he had ever heard in his life.

And even though she'd reacted as if it were ridiculous, to see him react the same way, to imply that the idea of them was stupid, hurt her. But she couldn't show it. She forced a smile and poked at her food.

The beef wellingtons were delicious as always, but Lorna was filled with a strange discomfort. She was a habitual people pleaser, and it did not sit well with her that Jo might not have liked her. She'd always imagined that Jo was fine with her spending time with Oliver. She'd been helping him get through med school. He wouldn't have passed without her. And surely Jo would have *wanted* him to pass? 'I wish I could have spoken with her. Put her mind at rest.'

'I think her doubts came from her mindset that she was missing out. The chemo made her feel so ill, she would barely leave the house most days, but she saw me going out, participating in life, following my dream and I was doing all of that with a girl? A girl that wasn't her? I could see her point of view, honestly.'

Lorna nodded. 'You were put in a difficult position. I'm sorry if our friendship made your life much harder than it needed to be.'

He shrugged. 'It's in the past. We got through it. What about you? What happened between you and Craig?'

Lorna sucked in a deep breath and then let it out again. In some ways, her history was similar to Oliver's. 'We were great. Until he cheated on me.'

'Really?'

'We went through a similar thing. We got married, everything was great, then we began trying for a family, starting as you do with all that youthful exuberance and belief that it will probably just take a few months, but then a year went past and then another without a single blip in my cycle. My period came every month, on time, as expected. But I lived in hope and kept buying tests and doing them early, only for them to come out negative.

'We decided to consult the doctors. They performed tests and discovered I had a hostile uterus, which is a phrase any woman just loves to hear.' A hostile uterus meant that the mucus that existed in her uterus was not the best when it came to swimming sperm that might want to go find an egg to burrow through. It would prevent the sperm from moving and sometimes be so acidic as to kill them. 'So we embarked on IVF as well.'

'You did?' Oliver looked intrigued.

She nodded. 'They implanted two embryos on the first round we did. It failed. The second round, they implanted two more. We got a positive pregnancy result from that one and we were so excited. Well, *I* was. Craig seemed a little distant, but I put it down to the whole exhaustive process. I finally thought our dreams might have come true, that everything would be all right now and Craig and I would be close again, but we performed an early ultrasound at week eight and there was no heartbeat.'

'I'm so sorry.'

Lorna smiled, refusing to revisit the pain of that moment, and forced herself to carry on with her own sad tale. 'We tried a third time. There was one embryo left and we pinned all our hopes on it. *I* pinned all my hopes on it. We were at work when the blood results came through. I took the call and discovered that we had failed and was devastated, I went looking for Craig to tell him the news. I found him in his consulting room with his tongue down the throat of one of our receptionists.'

Oliver looked at her in shock.

'That kind of ended things on a permanent basis.' She sipped her drink. 'I couldn't stay working in the same place as them. It was humiliating. I served my notice and got a job here. That was years ago and I've been happily single ever since.' She raised her glass, hoping she sounded convincing. She was happy. Mostly. But she did often feel lonely.

He clinked it, thoughtful. 'I can't believe we both went through similar struggles. If we'd have known we could have helped each other through it.'

Lorna nodded. 'Maybe we could have.' She thought of what that might have looked like. Weekly calls? Fortnightly? Jo would probably have hated that too. Lorna remembered all too well what it felt like to have her hormones played with. She'd become so emotional sometimes, not knowing whether she was coming or going. One moment she could be laughing at something, the next in floods of tears. Her nerves had been on a knife edge and anything could have set her off.

Feeling Craig drift away from her had felt awful. That feeling of suspecting you were losing someone and not being able to do anything about it…it was horrible. Losing a chance of a family every month. Losing her embryos with every implantation. Losing her husband… Especially when you felt as if you were doing everything to keep yourselves together. To try and grow a family for that person. To have a baby in the hope that everything would be right again. She should have known. Should have stopped the process and sorted her *relationship* first, then maybe she wouldn't have gone through so much in the first place? But she'd ploughed on, believing that a positive result on a pregnancy test would somehow set the world back on its axis.

'They're still together, Craig and Anya, the receptionist. They've got kids, so it all worked out for him, at least.' She tried not to sound bitter. Because she wasn't. Not really. Not any more, anyway. It was more of a wry assessment.

'He clearly was not the right person for you.'

'No.' So who was? She looked at him from across the table, her heart going pitter-patter. Once upon a time she'd yearned to believe that Oliver was the person for her, but he had been with someone else.

Maybe I just have a habit of choosing the wrong man?

Oliver felt a strange surge of unexpected anger when he heard what Craig had done to Lorna. Cheating on her when she was trying to get pregnant with their child? The man sounded like scum. No honour at all. No pride. No moral centre. No idea of sacrifice. Whilst Lorna was going through so much.

Oliver knew what IVF cycles were like. They

were long and arduous. Tough to get through. He'd watched Jo go through everything, because most of it fell upon the woman. All the guy had to do was provide a sample and that was no hardship, but the woman? She had to face tracking of her cycle, artificially *changing* that cycle, flooding the body with hormones, enduring daily injections, examinations, scans, procedures.

Jo had once suffered horrendously with a condition called ovarian hyperstimulation syndrome. Her abdomen had swollen, she'd felt sick, vomited, suffered dehydration and fluid had begun to build in her chest, affecting her breathing. When she'd been admitted into hospital and told to stop her IVF for a while, they had been devastated.

But Craig had thought nothing of his wife's sacrifice and cheated behind her back, humiliating her in front of her work colleagues.

If I ever meet that man, I'll have a few harsh words to say.

He wished he could have saved Lorna that pain. Maybe if they hadn't lost touch with one another, he could have? Maybe both of their lives would have been different? He'd never told anyone about how he'd once been thinking of ending things with Jo before they'd discovered her cancer. How their relationship had been flailing and in the weeds for a while. He'd been building up to it. Thinking about how he could do so without hurting her. He'd wanted them to remain friends, if possible.

But then things between them had got a little better and he'd discovered that lump when they were in Paris...then she'd been having investigations and been extremely nervous and worried. He couldn't have left her like that. What kind of a human being would he have been?

And so he'd stayed. Stuck by her side. Through thick and thin. Supported her. Cared for her. Advocated for her. Loved her as best he could and, yes, the fight to live, the fight against a cruel disease, had brought them back together. It had made them stronger when it could tear others apart, and he'd been so happy when she'd finally got the all-clear, of course he'd said yes to her proposal of marriage, because they'd been through so much by then, he'd thought nothing could tear them apart. The fight, the sacrifices, would not be for nothing. And he had really wanted a child and he had loved Jo.

But now? Looking back? He was glad that they hadn't had children together, because if they had, then he wouldn't have gone travelling, he wouldn't have found himself, he wouldn't have looked for his own happiness, he'd be continuing to sacrifice it for others. He wouldn't be sitting where he was right now, and right now felt wonderful. Because he was back with Lorna and looking at her face and seeing her smile. Hearing her voice was like a balm to his soul.

The lavender and honeycomb cheesecake was placed before them and he took a bite, not sure if the two flavours would be a good combination, but, oh, my goodness, they worked! And he polished off the dessert as quickly as he could.

'Convert?' Lorna asked.

'Absolutely. They make that here? I'm coming back every night, just for this.'

Lorna laughed. 'Actually, it's from Verity's. She makes all the local cheesecakes. Ships them all over the world. They're famous.'

'I'm not surprised. This ought to be in everyone's staple diet.'

'I don't think that would make for a healthy population.'

'Probably not, but think of all the running you could do afterwards to burn it off.' He smiled.

'You still run?'

'I do. Not as often as I should. In fact, I only started up again recently. I've been meaning to do it more often. What about you? I remember you used to run.'

'I still do. I run to work every day and again in the evenings, if I can. In fact, I'm training for the local marathon. I'm raising money for a stillbirth charity after one of my patients lost a child.'

That had to be awful. 'I'm sorry to hear that. What's the marathon?'

'It's called the Clear Twenty-Six. The route takes you all around the local area, through Clearbrook and all the other neighbouring villages. It's a mix of road and trail running. Lots of elevation, so I'm not sure I'll make it.' She laughed nervously, sounding uncertain. Unsure of herself. 'But if I have to crawl across the finishing line on my hands and knees, which, frankly, is probably going to be very likely, then I'll do it.'

'When is it?'

'Soon!' She took a sip of her drink, nervous of how fast the time was approaching.

'Fancy a training partner? I'm an experienced runner. I ran a half marathon just a month ago and I've been building up my distances. I could accompany you.'

She looked shocked. 'You mean that?'

'Absolutely! I could do with losing some of this.' He patted his stomach.

'There's nothing there to lose!' she said.

'I'm wearing a very expensive girdle.' He winked.

Lorna laughed and he couldn't help but smile at her amusement. She was so lovely. He'd missed her so much. 'I'd love to train with you. When's your next run?'

'Tomorrow evening after work. Just a short one.'

'Then, if you're happy for me to join you, I will. And I'll sign up to run the marathon as well.'

She looked surprised. Pleased. 'You could run for a charity, too.'

He liked making her smile. 'I'll pick one.' He raised his glass for another toast. 'Running partners.'

She clinked his glass. 'Running partners.'

CHAPTER THREE

'I THINK I'M having TIAs.'

TIAs were transient ischaemic attacks or mini strokes. Oliver raised an eyebrow at his patient. An older gent, in his seventies. Walter McCormack. 'And what makes you think that, Mr McCormack?'

'Call me Walt, please. I have these episodes, I guess you could call them.'

'Can you describe them for me?'

'They're all a little different, to be fair.'

'Okay. So tell me about the last one you had.' Oliver glanced at Walt's medical history on the screen. There was a history of high blood pressure. Type two diabetes that was being controlled. He'd had a left knee replacement last year.

'I woke up in the night to use the bathroom. I had a wee, washed my hands and the next thing I knew, I was on the floor. I tried to stand, but my arm and leg on my right-hand side wouldn't work properly. It was like they were weak and

I struggled to get to my feet. I had to call my wife to help me.'

'And when was this?' There was no mention of a hospital visit in Walt's records.

'Last week.'

'And you didn't call for an ambulance?'

'Well, no. I felt okay by the time I got back to the bedroom and I didn't want to worry my wife. Sheila? She's not well.'

'Did you bang your head when you fell?'

'I don't think so. I didn't feel any lumps or bumps and I didn't have a headache.'

'And you didn't feel dizzy or unwell whilst you were washing your hands?'

'I think I remember my eyesight feeling weird. Fuzzy. Like I couldn't focus, but it was fine when I was on the floor, because I remember noticing there was a loo roll behind the sink.'

Oliver nodded, thinking. 'How long do you think you were on the floor for?'

'Well, I went to the bathroom about two a.m., maybe just before, and by the time I got back to the bedroom it was ten past, so not long.'

'And do you think you lost consciousness?'

'I don't know.'

'Okay, well, I'd like to perform a set of observations, if that's all right with you?'

'Of course, Doctor.'

Oliver performed a series of checks. Blood

pressure. Temperature. Checked Walt's ears using his otoscope to see if he had an ear infection. His vision and eye movements. Strength. Reflexes. Heart rhythm. Everything was coming back normal. Nothing out of the ordinary. 'And you say you've had a few of these episodes?'

Walt nodded. 'I had one at my daughter's a month or so ago. We'd gone to visit the grandkiddies after school. I was just sitting in my chair, chatting to the youngest, when my daughter said I went blank for a moment.'

'Like you weren't present?'

'Exactly, but in my mind, I'd been there, present all the time.'

It did sound as though something neurological was going on with Walt, but the events had happened last week and before that, so there was nothing Oliver could do right now. It certainly sounded possible that he could be having TIAs, or mini strokes, that were not leaving any lasting deficits afterwards. 'All right, well, it does sound like something's going on. Whether you're having TIAs or not, I can't say for sure. Not without witnessing one personally or getting you into hospital within an hour of one happening. But I'd like to keep an eye on this, so why don't we meet up again in, say, a month? If you have any more then we can refer you to a neurologist for an assessment, but if not, then we can see how we go. How does that sound?'

'Sounds good to me.'

When Walt had gone, Oliver updated his records and checked his watch. Time for a cuppa. He checked Lorna's list. She didn't appear to be with a patient at the moment and so he went to her door and rapped his knuckles upon it.

'Come in!'

He opened the door and smiled. 'Making a brew. Want one?'

'Oh! You're a star! Tea, please.' She passed him her mug. It was red and had words on it that read *World's Best Doctor.*

He raised an eyebrow. 'Gift?'

'From a very grateful patient, not because I'm egotistical and bought it for myself.'

'I would never have considered that. What did you do?'

'I diagnosed her Addison's disease, when her last doctor kept dismissing her symptoms as anxiety.'

'Addison's? Good catch.' Addison's disease was an adrenal insufficiency that could cause stomach issues, weakness, weight loss and sometimes darkening of the skin.

'I can't believe her last doctor missed it. She had classic symptoms. He could have caught it with a simple set of blood tests.'

'How do you have it?'

'What?'

'Your tea. Last I remember, it was milk with one sugar.'

She smiled at him. 'It still is.'

He was glad she hadn't changed. In fact, the more time he spent with Lorna, the more he realised she was still the same woman he had always known. Only age and time had tried to change her. The self-doubt was still there.

'Coming right up.'

He quickly made them both tea, then took her filled mug back to her room and passed it to her. 'How's your morning going?'

'I've seen a nasty abscess, a case of chicken pox, one urine infection and a sore throat. How about you?'

'Back pain, migraines, an ear infection and a possible case of TIAs.'

'Who?'

'Walt McCormack.'

She nodded. 'Bless him. I hope it's not that. He's a carer for his wife, Sheila.'

'I'm keeping an eye out for him. Told him to call if he experiences anything strange.'

'Are you still up for our run tonight?' she asked, looking at him as if she'd expected him to back out.

'Absolutely. Where are you taking me?'

Lorna blushed and he had to admit he liked it. She looked beautiful. The tilt of her head, the soft flush in her cheeks. 'Through the woods and up to the lavender fields and back. It's a nice run. Slight elevation. Five kilometres. Road and trail, which is what we need to practise on.'

'Sounds perfect. I signed up for the marathon online when we got back from our meal.'

'Have you chosen a charity?'

'Yes. It's a group that supports families through infertility.' He knew they'd both had their struggles there. It seemed apt.

'That sounds great.'

'They do a lot of good work. They run a twenty-four-hour helpline that anyone can ring and just be listened to when they're feeling upset or frustrated, angry or confused.'

'I certainly remember feeling all of those things.'

'Yeah. Me too.' He'd wished he had somewhere to reach out when he and Jo had been going through all of that. But back then, there'd been nothing like that. And he'd felt as though all their friends had heard enough about either Jo's illness or their issues getting pregnant and he'd not wanted to lean on them any more than they already had. And so he'd kept a lot of his frustrations and upsets to himself. Trying to be strong for Jo. But because he'd done that, withdrawing into himself, Jo had felt him pulling away and it had simply restarted all their old arguments. The ones they'd had before she'd even begun to get sick. Her jealousy. Her insecurities rising to the surface. Accusing him of flirting with the women at work, which had been blatantly untrue. Oliver was not and could *never* be a cheat.

'Did you ever feel alone with it all?' he asked. It was the one thing he'd felt above all else. Even though he knew that there were thousands, if not hundreds of thousands of people around the globe that faced the same thing.

'Too much. Even though I had all these people focused on me. Doctors. Nurses. Specialists. Family members. All watching me. Waiting. Expecting things. For my temperature to be a certain number, for my hormone levels to be within a certain range. For my ovaries to produce a certain amount of eggs. So much focus and yet… I felt alone. Like I was failing them all when my body didn't respond the way they expected it to. Feeling less of a woman. When I failed month after month to give Craig's parents the grandchild they so desperately wanted, I felt their pity, their sympathy and, after a while, their dismissal. Like they'd given up on me and I was a failure. They'd never been my biggest fans and I felt certain they were telling Craig to look elsewhere. It took me a long time to get past the feeling that I had failed them all. I'm still not sure I have now.'

Oliver stared at her. 'You're not a failure.'

'Thank you. But when you tell yourself something, or hear it from others often enough, it's hard to get past it.'

'Then get ready, because I'm going to start telling you how amazing you are. Every single day. Until you believe it.'

She smiled at him. '*You're* amazing.'

He winked. 'But not as amazing as you.'

Her day began to feel a little better after that. Oliver's kind words, his attentiveness to her well-being, kept making her smile at odd moments during the day. She really could have done with his relentless optimism and cheerleading whilst she was going through infertility with Craig—though she wasn't sure that Craig would have loved her best friend being a guy. She might have got through it all so much easier with Oliver by her side.

She thought about their dinner together at Jasper's. How he'd walked her home afterwards to make sure she got there safely, even though she'd told him he didn't have to. 'Clearbrook isn't exactly filled with rapists and killers, you know,' she'd said.

'What about muggers and thieves? Any of those?'

'Not that I've heard of.'

'How about a really mean cat?'

Lorna had laughed. 'Now you mention it, Mr Penrose's Maine Coon has a bit of a temper!'

They'd reached her front door and she'd turned. Asked him if he wanted to come in for coffee.

He'd glanced at his watch. 'It's late and it's a school night. I'd better go. There'll be hell to pay with my boss and colleagues if I'm late tomorrow, and I need my beauty sleep.' He'd winked.

Of course. She was being too much. He'd probably had enough of her today. She would have liked him to come in for coffee. Just to spend a bit more time with him. He always made her feel better about everything.

'Regrettably, yes. Goodnight, Lorna.' And he'd leaned in to drop a kiss upon her cheek.

Thinking of that kiss now, as she waited for him to turn up for their first training run together, she couldn't help but think about how her body had responded to it. To his leaning in, to his lips pressing against her skin, the casual way his hand had rested upon her waist as he'd done so. The heat of him. The proximity of him. Her body had wanted more. Just as it had when they'd been younger. She'd always been attracted to Oliver and it looked as if that attraction hadn't gone away. Her body had still reacted to him. Her heart had beat faster. Her blood pressure had risen. Her mouth had gone dry. Her skin had tingled to his touch.

But it was probably best that they stayed just friends now. What could she offer him? They'd both wanted to be parents and she was in the thick of menopause now, whereas Oliver could still have children if he picked the right partner, which, obviously, wouldn't be her. And even though both of them were single, she didn't want to risk trying anything and it blowing up in her face. She'd dated and married a colleague before, and look at how badly that had turned out for her.

She was settled here in Clearbrook and it sounded as if Oliver was looking for somewhere to settle too. To create that longevity with patients that spanned years and decades. She couldn't put that at risk. For either of them.

They'd both been through the mill. Both had fought infertility and lost. Both divorced. Both were wary of anything new. But Oliver had a chance now to grab what he couldn't achieve before. The chance of a family. If he still wanted one, even if he would be an older father.

So, best to be just friends.

It was better for both of them.

* * *

Lorna looked amazing in her running gear. She wore a black tee, emblazoned with the name of a band he'd never heard of, and black running leggings that moulded to her form and revealed her shapely legs and rear, the latter of which he only noticed because when he arrived to join her, she had her back to him and was tightening the laces on her trainers.

He'd never seen her in anything tight before. Lorna had always hidden her shape behind baggy oversized hoodies, jeans or scrubs borrowed from the hospital. There'd been hints, of course. A stance, a turn, that had *suggested* a shapely figure beneath the clothes, but he'd never really seen it and to see it now? Well…there was certainly a reaction. He felt it, but hid it behind an ebullient greeting and a great show of arranging his water pouch in his running vest.

'Have you warmed up?' Lorna asked, once they'd both said hello and greeted one another with a kiss upon the cheek. Her skin was soft. Creamy. Her hair smelt of flowers.

'Not properly.'

'We should do some stretches before we begin. To prevent injury.'

And so he followed her lead, trying to focus on her directions rather than the way she looked and most definitely trying to not focus on how much he'd rather admire her. He didn't normally stretch, even though he knew he ought to, but now he actually enjoyed it. Once they were warmed up, they set off on their run.

Lorna led them through the village on the roads, before turning and heading onto the trail that ran through the woods, and she increased their speed to a good pace.

As soon as they left the village and they were surrounded by woods and birdsong and the scent of mulch and greenery, he felt himself relax even more. Even Lorna slowed. This place was perfect. A green canopy above, sunlight filtering through the gaps, the earth sparkling with sunbeams. He saw a squirrel dart up the trunk of a horse-chestnut tree and off to his left he even saw a small group of muntjac deer dart away through the undergrowth. Oliver couldn't help but smile.

'Doing okay?' Lorna asked as they jogged.

'Yep. You?'

'Doing great!' She gave a small burst of speed and he laughed, catching up with her, running alongside her once again. 'This feels great after sitting down in clinics all day.'

'Blows away the cobwebs for sure,' he agreed as they broke into an open glade briefly, before heading back beneath the cover of the trees. 'I don't think I've ever run anywhere so beautiful as this.'

'Just you wait.' Lorna veered away from the main trail and down to the left, following a smaller, thinner path.

He followed, trusting her, and soon he could hear the bubbling of water as Lorna brought them to a trail that ran alongside a small, babbling brook, which in turn led to a small, but ancient set of stepping stones that led across it. They slowed, crossed the water carefully and when they got to the other side, Lorna leaned forward to take deep breaths. Hands on her knees.

'You okay?'

She nodded.

'Didn't set out too hard?'

'Maybe a little. I just need a breather before we head up there.'

The trail led sharply upwards to where he could see a break in the trees and bright sunshine.

'Take a drink. Get some fluids on board.'

She followed his direction. 'Can you believe we're doing this? Sometimes, I think I'm crazy to even think I can tackle a marathon.'

'You've done harder things than this.'

'Like what?'

'Got through doctor training and God knows

how many rounds of IVF, in which your body wasn't your own. You're a lot stronger than you give yourself credit for.'

'Am I?'

'Yes. You are. Come on. The secret is to just keep putting one foot in front of the other.'

They set off again, huffing and puffing up the steep track, and when they reached the top of the hill, she stopped again to admire the view. Like a reward.

They'd reached the lavender fields. A mass of purple from the lightest lilac to the darkest plum, in long, neat rows. The flowers covered the fields in perfectly straight lines, waving gently in the evening breeze, and seemed to stretch for miles. These were the famous lavender fields of Clearbrook and they were astonishingly beautiful. His nostrils filled with their scent and he couldn't help but reach out and pluck a stem from a plant and hold it to his nose. 'Wow.'

'Isn't it amazing? I come up here often, whenever I'm feeling stressed. It always helps me.'

'I can see why.' There were lots of bees here. He could see them buzzing from flower to flower, collecting pollen, and he also glimpsed a few rabbits over to the left of the field darting into the low hedgerows. He pulled out his mobile phone from his vest pocket and took a photo to remind him of this moment. 'Let's get one of us together.'

She laughed. 'Really?' And stepped to his side.

He switched the camera on his phone to face view and draped an arm around Lorna's shoulder as they took a selfie with the lavender fields behind them. They both looked happy. Healthy. Hearty. Their faces infused with colour from their run. He showed her the picture afterwards.

'Oh, I love that! Will you send me a copy?'

'Sure. I'll message you. Want to give me your number?'

She reached for his phone, tapped it in and blushed as she handed it back.

He sent her a copy and smiled, sliding his phone back into his vest pocket.

'Over there, behind the hedgerows, are the apiaries. George Shanahan, who farms these fields, keeps bees and sells the honey that they make.'

'I bet it tastes amazing.'

'You can buy it anywhere in the village and Verity uses it in a honey cheesecake that will blow your mind.'

'I'll add it to my list of things to try.'

She smiled. 'Ready to head back?'

'Lead the way.'

It seemed to take less time to make their way back to the village in that strange way that time worked whenever you headed for home and before he knew it they were back at the village, at the green where they'd met, and Lorna was leading him through some cooling-down exercises and stretches. When they were done, they both had a long drink of water. 'One run down, only a gazillion to go.'

'Have you ever run a marathon before?' he asked.

'No. Just park runs and five-kilometre races. This is a huge challenge for me. What about you?'

'I managed that half marathon I told you about and a few charity runs. I discovered it's not just about the physical training you do, the practice runs, but the mental game as well. You hit a wall out there on a long run and you need the mental fortitude to push past it and know that you can keep going, when all you want to do is stop.'

'I hear that. But at least we'll have each other for support. Should be easier than going it alone.'

'Absolutely.' He nodded. 'What are you doing for the rest of your evening?'

'Going home and having a long bath. Then I'll grab myself something to eat and watch a movie, maybe, before heading to bed.'

It sounded great. He would have loved to join her, he realised, in all of those things. And the idea of joining Lorna in the bath flashed into his brain and wouldn't go. That would certainly throw a spanner in the works. He laughed nervously and raised a hand in a goodbye, knowing he couldn't do that. Lorna was his friend. His lifelong friend. He wasn't looking for another relationship in which he had to make sacrifices and give control over to another person again. He still wanted time to be a little selfish. Control his own life, without constantly having to worry about someone else.

'Sounds perfect. Well, I'd better go. You have a good evening and thanks for today.' He leaned in to kiss her goodbye. Closed his eyes to savour the brief moment his lips pressed against her cheek and he breathed her in. But he knew he was doing the right thing in stepping away. He didn't ever want his life to be curbed by anyone else again; it was his time now and he was going to enjoy it. They already worked together all day long and now they trained together. That was enough.

Even if he was still curious about her life.

Her place would no doubt be perfect. Softly furnished. Warm. Welcoming.

The cottage that he'd rented was still filled with boxes that he hadn't unpacked. He'd not yet made the place his home—he'd been working a lot. Maybe at the weekend he could put some effort into getting rid of them, unpacking and settling into his new place?

He turned to check that she was walking back to her place. Saw her reach for her ponytail and release her wave of auburn hair, so that it cascaded over her shoulders and down to her mid-back like a fiery waterfall, glinting and catching the sunlight.

Lorna was beautiful. She'd always been beautiful.

But she didn't know it. Wasn't aware of it.

And it was something he longed to show to her.

To prove to her.

He wanted her to know that he saw her in that way.

CHAPTER FOUR

VERITY WAS BACK and she'd been seen by the hospital. 'It's cancer.' Verity sat in front of her looking pale and numb. Her normally perfect appearance a little off kilter. No make-up. An old sweatshirt with jeans. Her hair falling out of its clip. 'I never thought it would be. I'd convinced myself it was a cyst.'

'I'm so sorry, Verity. Have they said what their next steps are?'

'I've got to have all these scans. Bloodwork. I've got an appointment with an oncologist coming up, but I just feel kind of stunned all the time. Like I can't take anything in at all.'

'You're in shock. I think that's a perfectly reasonable reaction to what you've just learned.'

'Jack and I were going to go on a second honeymoon before all of this, did you know that?'

Lorna shook her head.

'We never really got a first one. I was working hard to get the business off the ground and so we were working all hours, what with the online boom we had after that article in that American newspaper about a little ole cheesecake shop in England. We'd planned this itinerary. We were going to go to Marrakech, Tunisia, North Africa and travel our way down to the south and go on safaris in Kenya and Gambia. Jack wanted to fit in Madagascar, too. We'd spent hours trolling websites and writing down what we wanted to do. But because I felt so unwell, I thought it best to get checked out first. I just figured I was a bit anaemic or something. That all I'd need was a few iron tablets and I'd be sorted. But now we're facing this.'

As Lorna listened, she couldn't help but reflect on how Jo's cancer diagnosis had affected Oliver back in the day. They'd had dreams too. Oliver had already been in medical school training to be a doctor. Jo had been at uni training to be a vet. Jo had insisted that Oliver continue to attend uni, and she remembered one night turning up to the library for a study session with Oliver and how he'd arrived looking stressed and bummed out.

'Hey, what's up?' she'd asked.

'You don't want to know.'

'Oh. Okay.'

He'd sighed, run his hands through his thick, lush hair that had not yet been peppered with grey.

'Jo's just frustrated, is all. What do they say

about the seven stages of grief? I think she's in the anger stage.'

'She's allowed. Cancer has derailed all her dreams. She's had to press pause on her life and you get to carry on.'

'But I'm not though. I feel like my life has been paused, too.'

He'd told her then that Jo had trashed her little study area in anger. Thrown her textbooks and folders all over the place. Torn up some of her printed essays. How he'd told Jo that he'd take a break too, if it would make her feel better, and how she'd lost her mind at that. How she'd said that then he'd blame her for putting his life on hold too, and how she'd thrown her keyboard at the wall. How he'd walked over to her, pulled her into his arms to give her time to calm down and how she'd struggled in his arms, crying.

'It's not fair, Olly! It's not fair!'

'If you need a break, you can always stay at mine. There's room on the couch,' Lorna had suggested, blurting it out without even thinking about it.

He'd looked at her then with such longing that she'd felt something shift inside. An awareness. That maybe he'd felt something for her too. Had been seeing her in a different light, the way she'd wanted! But then a darkness had clouded his eyes and her hope had faded.

'Thanks, but me sleeping over at another girl's place won't help. Let's just get on with our studies. Learning about brain chemistry isn't going to happen by itself.'

And the subject had been closed. She'd seen and observed snippets like that through the years they'd studied together. Oliver and Jo would be fine and then there'd be a huge upset. A row. A slamming of a door. Jo would get frustrated with her treatment and the side effects. The way life had been happening for everyone else, whilst she'd felt stuck in limbo. It had been understandable and Lorna had wished she could do more for both of them, but she hadn't known how back then.

Not really. She'd just had hope. That life for Oliver and Jo would get easier. Cancer didn't affect just the person that had it, but those all around them.

She looked at Verity, wondering if she was going through the same thing. 'I know it's hard, but I'm always going to be here for you as you fight this and I know you'll fight hard. Let's arrange a standing appointment with each other. Every month, we'll meet and check in. Just to chat. To touch base. If you need me for anything other than that, you call and make an appointment—I will always be there for you, okay? I'll let the receptionists know to always fit you in.'

'Thanks, Lorna. And thank you for seeing me today.'

'No problem. If Jack needs to come in with you or by himself, tell him I'm just one phone call away, okay?'

'Thank you.'

'No problem. You take care of yourself.' She gave Verity a hug and waved her goodbye, watching her slumped, almost defeated form leave her room.

Cancer. Such a horrible, insidious disease. It wrecked so many lives. Touched so many people. Good people, who didn't deserve it. Young and old. Rich or poor. It wasn't selective. But when it happened, it did make people take stock. Made them realise what was important to them. Made them focus on what they wanted to achieve in life. Places they'd always wanted to go. Sights they'd always wanted to see. People that they needed to talk to. To clear the air. Or apologise, or simply say *I love you*.

Cancer made you realise what was important. It wasn't that you didn't know it before, it was just that the disease gave you *clarity*. Knowing you could die from it. Time became shorter. More important. More focused.

Since Oliver had started here, life had been amazing. It was great having him back in her life. Working together, running together. It was as if they'd always been together. As if they hadn't had decades of being apart. He perked her up. And Clearbrook Medical Practice was getting into a new rhythm with all of its new doctors. Lorna had spent time now with Bella and Max. They were both lovely and she actually suspected that there might be a bit of an attraction between the two of them. She couldn't be sure, but she wasn't usually wrong. They had a lot in common. Both of them single parents, with children the same age, in the same class. They lived opposite one another, having rented the two holiday cottages from Dr Mossman. Both young, working together. Living opposite one another... She'd seen the side eyes. The looks when they thought no one else was watching.

It was easier to see it in someone else than it was to see it in herself. Even though she knew she still held strong feelings for Oliver, they were both keeping each other firmly in the friend zone. The colleague and training-partner zone. It was safer that way. She couldn't be anything else to him and she wanted him to have options. Her childbearing days were over and she couldn't enter another romantic relationship. Not now. Not that she thought that Oliver would want to, but she didn't want to ever make herself small again to fit in with someone else.

He'd never been available to her before and

he wasn't now either. He'd always been with Jo and so her unrequited love for him had been something she could secretly treasure and nurture without harm. It hadn't ever been going to get her hurt, because he would never have been in a position to reject her romantically. It was better to have certainty and a deep love through friendship than it was to have *uncertainty* in a relationship.

But she couldn't escape the fact that he was here and they were both single. Both divorced. Both having gone down the infertility track. They had more in common now than they had ever had.

But she was scared to love Oliver again. Scared to open that box. Because she'd been cheated on. She'd been found wanting and Craig's betrayal had made her feel small. It had happened over time. Slowly. Because in the beginning, everything had been marvellous. The early years of their marriage had been the happiest she'd ever had. She'd felt as if her life were charmed, even if she had changed bits of herself to fit in with him and his family.

They'd told her in no uncertain terms that she wasn't Craig's usual type. That he'd always dated buxom blondes, women with hourglass figures, whereas she was slim, small and a redhead. She'd dyed her hair once and Craig had been appalled and made her take it back to its natural tones. She'd always loved going to the theatre or the cinema, but Craig hadn't and so they'd never gone. She'd liked the idea of having skiing holidays, but he'd always wanted sunshine, so they'd always ended up in the Mediterranean.

But it had been little things, too. Changing her choice of drinks. Changing her make-up. Him giving his opinion on her clothes. Her nails. Bit by bit, he'd slowly chipped away at her and she hadn't noticed. Not properly. Not until after the relationship was over.

And then of course he'd had that affair with a curvy blonde and she'd felt second best. Not good enough. And that was a hard thing to get over.

She was ruminating on these thoughts when Oliver knocked on her consulting room door and brought her in her tea. He'd got into the habit. Morning break, he'd make her tea and bring it to her and they'd chat in her room. Afternoon breaks, they'd be more sociable and take their breaks in the main staffroom with Bella, Max, Priti and whichever of the nurses were free.

Lorna loved these moments and tried her very best to keep them work-related as much as she could. 'I had a patient come back in today. She's just been diagnosed with cancer.'

'I'm sorry to hear that.'

'I wish I could do more for her, but it's out of my hands now.'

'Is this the lady who owns the cheesecake shop? I spoke on the phone to her husband, Jack, yesterday.'

'Yes.'

'He said he was struggling. I keep hearing about that cheesecake place, though. I must go one of these days.'

'Yes, we should support them. I could ring and book us a table.'

'You have to *book* to go to a cheesecake shop?'

'Well, yes. It's world-renowned and popular with tourists. The place is always packed, but maybe I'll be able to get a table.'

'Maybe I should run for two charities? Split the donations?'

She smiled at him. 'I don't see why not. That's a lovely idea.'

'I could run for a breast cancer charity. It makes sense, what with my history.'

'Jo.'

Lorna sipped at her tea and decided to change the subject. 'Did you have any interesting cases this morning?'

He shrugged. 'Not really. Run-of-the-mill stuff. Back pain. Headaches. A dodgy knee. I did see a case of pompholyx.'

'Oh. Okay.' Pompholyx was a type of eczema.

It caused blisters to form on the fingers and the palms of the hands and sometimes the soles of the feet. 'I've seen a couple of cases of that before. Not often, though.'

'I think it had been caused by stress. The patient had lost her job and was trying to raise her kids, whilst at the same time take care of her elderly parents.'

'The sandwich generation.'

'Mmm.' Oliver sipped at his tea. 'Where are we running this evening?'

'It's a longer run tonight, according to the training schedule. I thought we could run over to Todmore and back, though I might need oxygen assistance for that.'

'The next village over?'

'Yes. It's quite a scenic route. Mostly roads, though.'

'You'll do great. And when do we get the cheesecake?'

Lorna laughed. 'I'll give the place a call, see when a table is free.'

'Well, I never thought we'd get stopped by this.'

Oliver kept running on the spot as they waited for the farmer to transfer his flock of sheep from one field, across the road, to another field, whereas Lorna stopped, to catch her breath.

The animals filled the air with quite the fragrance as they baaed and bleated and jumped over imaginary obstacles on their way across the road, leaving a trail of mud behind. The farmer gave them both a wave of thanks as he closed the metal gate behind them and then he and Lorna were on their way again.

'Another hill? Fabulous!' she breathed.

'It's only a ten-per-cent incline. That's hardly anything,' he said, grinning.

'Doesn't make it easier.'

'You can do it!'

He could feel his leg muscles burning and his blood pumping as they neared the village of Tod-more. Lorna told him, breathlessly, that it was just over the hill, about another half-mile and then they'd be there. That they could use the old stocks on the village green as a midpoint to turn around at and head back. He took a sip of his water and nodded, unable to speak right now as the hill rose before them, twisting through the trees.

He kept his eyes on the horizon that he could see, willing himself to get there, knowing that once they breached the top, it would be so much easier running down the other side, but he wasn't sure if his eyes were deceiving him or not, be-cause he thought he could see some grey there amongst the blue sky that shone through the trees up ahead. Was that smoke? Or cloud? And what could he smell? Something metal. Something *burning*?

He glanced at Lorna to see if she'd noticed it too and realised that she was frowning as well. Somehow they picked up pace, sensing an urgency, and pushed the last fifty metres or so at speed, cresting the hill and stopping in shock at the sight of a car that had come off the road and hit a tree. Steam and something else were rising up from beneath the bonnet that was crumpled against a large tree trunk.

He and Lorna darted forward to render assistance. As they ran to the car, he pulled his mobile from his running vest and dialled 999 to ask for ambulance and the police. He recognised this car. It had passed them just after the sheep had, blaring music with a heavy bassline. He and Lorna had tutted about the youth of today, then laughed at how they'd both sounded like old fuddy-duddies and watched the car roar up the hill, slightly jealous of the ease with which the engine took the car up, knowing it would not be as easy for them on two sets of fifty-one-year-old legs.

Lorna edged her way through the nettles and undergrowth to reach the driver's door as Oliver finished relaying the details of their location and the incident to the emergency services. Then, once that was done, he pushed further through tried to turn to look at him, but cried out in pain and stopped.

'Where does it hurt?'

'My neck and my back.'

'Okay. My name's Oliver and this is Lorna. We're both doctors. I think you drove past us on the hill.'

'I don't remember.'

'How much have you both drunk?'

'I don't know. A couple of cans?'

'Of beer?'

She tried to nod, but cried out again.

Oliver reached in to support her neck. 'I don't want you to nod or turn your head. I want you to try and keep still until the paramedics get here, okay? They should be here soon. What drugs have you taken?'

'We haven't.'

'I can smell it in the car, Carmel. What have you taken and how much?'

'Just a spliff. One. I promise. We shared it.'

'Okay. Okay.'

'Mine's drifting in and out,' Lorna said.

Oliver glanced past Carmel towards Andy. Like him, Lorna was trying to maintain Andy's cervical spine—keeping his neck in a neutral position to protect his airway—but his head kept bobbing up and down and all the blood on his face was making it hard to see just what kind of

the undergrowth, jumping a ditch to ge
other side of the car to check on any oth
sengers.

'Stay awake for me,' he heard Lorna sa

Glancing at the driver, he saw a young
strapped into place behind the wheel, with b
running down his face from a large gash.
windscreen had been broken by a large protru
ing branch, that thankfully had come throug
the glass directly between the passenger an
driver. Either a little to the left or a little to th
right and one of them might have been impaled
in their seat. In the confines of the car, he could
smell alcohol and something sweeter. Marijuana.
The music continued to blare out from the speak-
ers, so he reached forward to punch the buttons
and silence it. The passenger, a young woman,
was trembling and shaking in her seat. The two
air bags had deployed, but they were both covered in small cuts and lacerations from the broken windshield.

The driver seemed to be losing consciousness, from the accident, the alcohol or drugs,
they couldn't know.

'What's your name?' he asked the young
woman, who had begun to cry.

'Carmel.'

'Okay, Carmel. And who is this next to you?'

'Andy. He's my boyfriend. Is he okay?' She

injuries he'd received. They couldn't check his skull for a fracture, but he was developing dark circles under his eyes, which was not a good sign. It could indicate a skull fracture.

'Any blood in his ears?'

'None that I can see from this side.'

'Nor my side.'

'Just maintain that C-spine and airway. It's all we can do right now.'

He was impressed with how calm Lorna was. She'd totally switched into doctor mode. She was focused, level-headed and in control. And she was talking to Andy in a low voice, even though neither of them knew if Andy was even conscious enough to be aware of her words. But she did it anyway. Trying to sound soothing. Telling him that help was on the way and that he'd be okay.

Eventually they began to hear sirens that got closer and closer and soon enough a large yellow ambulance was pulling up on the road. It parked at the crest of the hill and put on its hazard lights, so that any traffic coming up the hill wouldn't speed up it, only to be confronted by a crash site. It would save any further accidents from happening.

Oliver told the paramedics what he knew and then he and Lorna stepped back and let them take over, placing cervical collars on Andy and

Carmel. Their car doors still worked, so there was no need for any firemen to cut them out to get them placed on backboards, though firemen were now arriving, too.

'You okay?' Oliver asked Lorna.

'I'm fine. Well, apart from this little cut I got on my leg from going through that gorse bush, but I'm okay.'

He knelt to look at her leg and saw the cut. A small amount of blood had run down her calf towards her trainer. 'We'll get that sorted, don't worry.'

The first ambulance that had arrived had taken Carmel away already, as she'd been easily extracted first. Andy, as the more seriously hurt passenger, had been extracted second and now he was being loaded onto the emergency vehicle. Oliver knew he could have asked the paramedics for some gauze and saline for Lorna's leg, but they were busy sorting Andy and his injuries were more important, so he said nothing and watched them drive away. They gave statements to the police about what they'd witnessed and what Carmel and Andy had admitted to and then the police offered them lifts back to Clearbrook.

It felt strange being in the back of a police car.

But even stranger to be standing outside Lorna's cottage, watching her slide the key into the lock and invite him in.

He'd not been in before. They'd kept their relationship outside each other's homes since he'd been back in her life. They saw each other at work. They met in the village at a mutually agreed place before they started and ended their runs. Occasionally, they'd made it into a pub for a drink and their cheesecake date was coming up, which he knew wasn't a *date* per se. They'd meant to go before, but had been unable to secure a table. Verity had been so busy. Booked out, which was great for her business, whilst she'd begun her chemo.

'Come in. First-aid kit's in the kitchen.' She led him down a hallway and he glimpsed her living room and a downstairs bathroom briefly before he arrived in her kitchen. He'd heard of the term *'cottagecore'* before and, if he understood it correctly, her kitchen was a perfect example. A scrubbed stone floor, old wood units with gingham checked curtains, plates, cups and bowls stacked openly on a pastel-coloured dresser, each item mismatched, yet somehow perfectly matching its neighbours in colour or pattern. Lots of leafy green plants hung in corners: trailing ivy, spider plants, succulents. Herbs in pastel-coloured pots on the windowsill, glass jars full of cookies or flour, copper pans hanging from a rack above their heads. Something cooling on a wire rack, with a checked tea towel draped over it.

Strangely, he'd never imagined her as a baker, but now was wondering if she was the source of all the wonderful baked goods that seemed to always be in a tin in the staffroom at work.

'Here we go. Gauze. Saline. Plaster.'

'Let me.'

'It's okay. I can do it.'

'I know you can, but isn't it always nice when someone else does it?' He smiled at her, taking the items from her hands as she pulled out a chair and sat down.

'Go on, then.' She held her leg out in front of her.

Oliver sat opposite her with a smile. He picked up her leg and placed it on his lap.

She had very nicely toned legs, but now he could see nettle stings and other scratches on her calf from pushing through the undergrowth to get to the crashed car. Sharp pink lines, one or two that had beaded blood, though not as bad as the main laceration. And now, in the light of the kitchen, he thought he could see something.

'Do you have tweezers in that first-aid kit?'

'Yes. Why?'

'There's something in the cut. A splinter? Something like that.'

Lorna passed him the tweezers and he poured some saline over the wound first, before carefully using the tweezers to grab hold of the offending item and pull it out. A thorn. 'Wow.'

Oliver smiled at her. Impressed that she hadn't flinched or made a sound. In fact, she'd been rather stoical, which she continued to be as he examined the rest of the cut to see if there was any other offending material that ought not to be there, but it looked clean. He used the rest of the saline to wash it out and then dried it with the gauze pad, until the blood stopped running, and applied a plaster. 'There you go. Good as new.'

She lowered her leg to the floor. Turning it this way and that. 'Did anyone tell you that you could be an excellent doctor?'

'Someone might have mentioned it.'

'I bet you have a wonderful bedside manner.' She smiled at him, met his gaze and then something strange happened.

It was as if the mention of the words 'bedside manner' had somehow made her imagine him standing by her bed. Being near her bed. Sitting on her bed. Because she blushed and looked away, got up and immediately began to occupy herself by picking up a tea towel and wiping an already clean surface. 'Tea?' she asked, not looking at him now.

* * *

He tried not to think of how he'd feel if he were ever close to Lorna in a bed. Would her hair look deliciously ruffled on her pillow? Would she be wearing pyjamas, or would her shoulders and arms be bare, hinting at nakedness beneath? The very idea of a naked Lorna lying on her bed and looking up at him made him glad that he was sitting down.

'Tea would be great,' he managed, trying to pull his focus back to the real world by eyeing up the array of cookbooks she had on a shelf nearby. 'You, er…do a lot of baking?' He wasn't ready to think of Lorna in such a way. He was in no hurry to rush headlong into another complicated relationship, because that was what it would be, considering their history and the fact that they worked together. Imagine if it all went wrong? He didn't want that and he didn't want complicated, either. He'd had enough of complicated.

She turned, smiling, grateful for the topic change. 'I try! I made this lemon drizzle earlier.' And she removed the tea towel from the loaf tin that had been cooling on the rack. 'It's *sans* drizzle at the moment.'

'So it's you that makes all the cakes and things at work?'

'Not always me. The cupcakes are usually Mia.' Mia was one of the receptionists.

'Who did that white-chocolate brownie thing the other week?'

'White-chocolate blondie. That was me.'

'It was delicious!'

'Thank you.' She seemed genuinely thankful for his compliment and looked as if she wanted to say something else, but, whatever it was, she stifled it and returned to making the tea.

Now it was safe to stand up, he got up and had a look out of her kitchen window. Her back garden, though small, or *bijou* as an estate agent might call it, was packed with flowers around a tiny patio and seating area.

'Did you do all of that yourself, too?' He was learning so much about Lorna. Things he didn't know. Things he'd never found out about her when they were at medical school all those years ago. Back then, she'd been so focused on her studies. On revision. She'd always had a book in her hand, or a pen and paper, making meticulous notes and researching study methods. But what had he actually known about her? She'd been good at pub quizzes, he remembered that, with a seemingly unfathomable amount of trivia knowledge. She'd put it down to the fact that her dad used to watch a lot of quiz shows on television and she would sit with him. She'd never seemed into fashion or music, but she would talk about books. Had she always baked? Did she like to garden? What else did she like?

'I did. It was an overgrown jungle when I first moved in, but whenever the weather was nice and I wasn't at work, I'd chip away at it.'

'Laying the patio? Everything?'

'Mmm-hmm. You see that large black pot there, next to the seat?'

'Yes.'

'It's a goldfish pond.'

'You're kidding.'

'No. Come and see.' She led him outside through two old French doors and into her garden and, sure enough, the large flowerpot was filled with water, plants and two perfect white and orange goldfish inside.

'And you did this all by yourself, too?'

'It's amazing what you can learn on the Internet.' She laughed at his shocked expression.

She was a marvel. 'You really are a woman of many talents, aren't you?'

'Well, I wouldn't say that,' she answered, blushing, though clearly pleased that he could see all that she had achieved.

He stared at her in amazement. She was wonderful. Beautiful. A talented and caring doctor. A runner for charity. A baker. A gardener. A DIYer. Self-deprecating. Funny. Kind. Caring. A phenomenal friend. With gorgeous eyes that looked at him now as if she loved him as much as he loved her. As a very good friend, obviously. With a wide smile that was generous and hypnotic and made him want to smile too.

The urge to pull her towards him and kiss her was so strong, so overwhelming, that he almost couldn't breathe. He felt trapped by her. By the sudden pull of her. He could imagine doing it. Reaching out for her hand and pulling her close. Feeling her body up against his. There would be uncertainty in her eyes at first, but then they would fall into the kiss and it would be amazing...

Or...she might laugh and pull her hand free and ask him, *What are you doing?* She would be embarrassed, afraid. Not sure how to handle the situation and say that she had a busy day the next day and then it would be awkward at work and their friendship wouldn't be the same and...

Oliver pushed the impulse down. Swallowed hard.

I will not kiss her. I will not ruin what we have.

They weren't young any more. They weren't foolish and impulsive. They were adults. Grown-ups. People their age had grandkids.

'Well, this is all amazing.'

She looked around her, clearly pleased with his compliments. 'It was a lot of hard work, but when you do that, you get to reap the rewards, don't you?'

'You do.'

Lorna indicated the bench. 'Take a seat. I'll bring our tea out here.'

When she was in the kitchen, he let out a sigh and sank down onto the bench, thinking hard about life and the choices he'd made. He'd pushed to come here. Had pulled out all the stops to make sure he seemed to be the best candidate Priti could ever want for Clearbrook Medical Practice and all because he'd known Lorna was here.

What had been his *real* reason for that? What had been his intention?

To re-establish a decades-old friendship? To get his friend back?

Or had he *hoped* for something more? Without even thinking about the impact his return might have on her? Because he'd believed she was married. She might have been in a marriage that had lost the initial spark, but what if they had been comfortable? Happy? Settled, with grown-up children? Would he have caused issues in her marriage, the way Lorna had unwittingly caused problems in his relationship with Jo?

But he'd not thought of any of that. Not once. All he'd been able to think of was getting back in touch with the one woman whom he'd felt the most comfortable with. The one woman who had truly understood him. Who had seen his vulnerable side and given him her strength. If he was being honest with himself? Lorna made him feel good and he'd not felt good for a long, long time. Had he wanted her to see the new him? The free Oliver? The bachelor Oliver? And if so, why was that?

When Lorna came out with the tea and two slices of lemon drizzle cake on a tray, he smiled at her in thanks and resolved to himself that he would not use Lorna to make himself feel better. He'd suspected she might have liked him more than she'd ever let on and it had been a huge a boost to his ego to know that a woman like *her* might have had feelings for him.

But he wasn't a kid any more. He understood people. He knew how they had both been hurt by romantic relationships and he wouldn't do that to her. Or to himself. He'd never deliberately go out of his way to hurt her, of course not, but it happened in relationships. People got hurt. It was the way of the world.

He would never put Lorna in a position in which she felt uncomfortable. He would keep them strictly as friends and demand nothing more from her than that.

CHAPTER FIVE

OLLY WAS ACTING strangely since they'd come across that car accident. Lorna had felt him pull away from her and she wasn't sure why. Had he lost someone to a car accident? Were his nights haunted by bad dreams? She wanted to ask him, but she also didn't want to pry and, as his best friend, she also wanted to give him his space to work through whatever feelings he was having. He would tell her in his own time, when he was ready, but she just wanted him to know that she was there for him. She could be his comfort. His shoulder to cry on. She knew that, because she'd done it before.

So, that morning, at work, instead of waiting for him to bring her a cup of tea in their morning tea break, she made the tea and took it to his consulting room, knocking briefly on his door.

'Come in!'

Oliver was sitting at his desk, typing notes into the computer. He looked very handsome today. Dark trousers, soft pink shirt, open at the neck. He looked up at her in surprise. 'What's this?'

'I thought I'd bring you tea for a change. My last patient didn't show and I was free. I thought it might be nice to look after you.'

'That's very kind. Take a seat.' He indicated the patient's chair and she sat down with her own mug and had a brief look around the room. She'd not really been in here properly since Oliver had begun working in the practice. He had his certificates up on the wall. A couple of children's paintings and thank-you cards tacked to a noticeboard. On his desk was a photo in a frame.

She leant forward, expecting to see a picture of Jo, but it wasn't. It was Oliver, with two older people that she guessed were his parents. Surprised, she sipped her tea and waited for him to finish.

His fingers moved swiftly over the keyboard. Then he hit the Enter key and turned to face her as he grabbed his mug. 'Well, this is nice. Thank you again.'

'No problem. You're always looking after me.'

He smiled and sipped his drink.

'And I like looking after you. Looking out for you. Making sure you're okay. It feels right.'

'I'm all right.'

'Are you? You seem a little…distant lately.'

'Me? No. I'm fine.'

'You're sure? I'm here, you know. Anytime you need to talk, I'm here for you.'

'I know that. What's prompted this?'

She shook her head. 'I don't know. But since that accident we came across, you haven't been the same.' She actually felt as though she missed him. Even though he was right there. It had been like the old days. The two of them against the world. He would make her laugh and she would enjoy being within his orbit. The day of the accident had changed everything. There'd been a moment afterwards, when he'd been tending to her leg and she'd felt his hands upon her, taking care of her, and she'd felt as if her heart might explode out of her chest. And then again, later, out in the back garden, she'd thought for a moment that…well, that he might kiss her, but she must have been mistaken.

She often realised much later that she had mistaken a man's desires. She'd thought Craig had loved her as much as she'd loved him and she'd been wrong. She'd thought he was still interested in being with his wife, but it had all been fake. She'd never been with anyone else, how on earth could she be qualified to know what a guy wanted? And what did she have to offer? Really? Dried-up eggs. Menopausal. Not as young as she used to be. Her own husband, who'd once loved her, had traded her in for a newer, younger model.

'Oh. Well, there's nothing wrong. Honestly.'

'You're sure?'

'Yes.' He smiled at her. A genuine smile that lit up his eyes and she felt reassured for the first time. There he was. Her best friend.

'Okay. It's a day off running today and I've managed to get us a table at Verity's cheesecake shop at six. She does late nights once a week.'

'I'm looking forward to it.'

'Great.' And yet somehow she still felt on edge. As if he wasn't talking to her the way he usually did. That he didn't sit next to her in staff meetings and give her a nudge with his elbow, so she would look at him and smile. That he didn't randomly message her with a funny joke or meme he found on the Internet. That their conversations of late didn't seem as deep as they usually did. 'Well, I'll let you get on. Busy morning.'

'You've got your Well Woman clinic this afternoon, haven't you?'

She nodded.

'I've got a patient on my schedule who's coming in because she's having bleeding after sex. Would I be able to get you to take a look if she wants to be examined?'

'You don't want to do it?'

'I'm happy to, but I know she asked the receptionist for a female doctor and you and Bella were both booked up, so they put her into my clinic for the consult, but told her that she could have a female doc do the examination if necessary.'

'Sure. No problem.' Lorna headed back to her own consulting room, sat down at her screen and stared at it. Her next patient was already here. Quentin Chiles. A man in his seventies, who was here about not being able to sleep. There was nothing in his record to state that he'd had issues before, so she was curious as to what was happening.

Quentin came in and sat opposite. 'Hello, Doctor.'

'Hello there, how can I help you today?'

Quentin sighed. 'I'm struggling, Doctor.'

'Okay, why don't you tell me a little about that?'

'I've lived alone all my life. I've never married, never had kids. It's never worked out for me, you know, and I thought I was fine about that, but I've met this woman at the church who seems wonderful. We get on great, she's a woman of God, she's kind, she's funny. A good friend, but… I think she wants more from me. Romantically, if you know what I mean, and I'm too set in my ways to be getting into all of that. I have my routines. I'm happy. And I like her, but…she's asked me out and I said I'd think about it.

'But I'm getting stressed out about it and not sleeping very well, because if I say no, I'll hurt her feelings and I might lose my friend, but if I say yes, simply because I don't want to hurt her, when I'm not into it, then surely that's the wrong thing to do, too? I can't sleep over this. It's driving me nuts!'

She smiled at him in sympathy. This was more of a personal issue than a medical one, but perhaps he felt he didn't have anyone else to talk to about this. 'Have you considered talking to her about it? Tell her your worries? If she's as good a friend as you say she is, she'd probably be happy to listen to you.' Lorna felt for the guy and actually she didn't mind being his sounding board. Her afternoon wasn't jam-packed.

'That's not my way, Doctor. I was raised to believe that a man was a man and he didn't share his feelings with his significant other. She'll think me weak.'

'Are you sure?'

'The other thing is that she's a lot younger than me. By a good ten years and one of my good friends suggested she might be after my money. I have a good private pension and significant savings and she's always been, how to say this, less fortunate with money, if you get my drift?'

She nodded.

'The stress of it all is stopping me from sleeping and I need my sleep, Doctor. It's the one thing I look forward to of an evening.'

'Well, listening to you, it sounds like you want to say no and, if that's the case, honesty is the best policy here. Why not sit down with this lady, tell her straight, but say you value her friendship?'

'But what if she gets upset? She seems very keen.'

'Then she'll be upset for a while, but she'll get over it.'

'Is it really that simple?'

'Absolutely! If you're the friends that you say you are and she likes you as much as you say, then I'm absolutely sure that she will understand, even if she does feel a little disappointed. She will value your friendship more and still get to have you in her life.'

He nodded. 'Maybe. I've been trying to avoid giving her an answer. Sticking my head in the sand and trying to ignore it. I haven't been to church in two weeks!'

'Then it's time to go back. This is hurting you. Stopping you from attending church, giving you stress, stopping you from sleeping. Just be honest with her. She'll appreciate it more than you know.' He definitely didn't need sleeping tablets, anyway.

He nodded. 'Thank you, Doctor. I appreciate you giving me the time today.'

'No problem. You take care.'

When he was gone, she couldn't help but think of the parallels with her own life. She had done what she had advised Quentin to do. She had spoken to Oliver. Asked him if everything was okay and let him know that she was always going to be there for him. It was what friends did.

The only question was whether she felt that Oliver had responded to her with the truth.

Verity's Cheesecake Emporium was on the high street of Clearbrook. It had Georgian windows and on display were cake stands filled with a variety of cheesecakes in highly polished glass domes. And after they'd decided to come here, they had finally got a reservation. He saw strawberries, blueberries, honey, lavender. Toffee, banoffee, crème caramel and chocolate. Sumptuous deliciousness no matter where he looked, and he finally understood why this cheesecake shop was as world-famous as Lorna had informed him.

When he opened the door, a little bell rang above his head and he was surprised to see the place was absolutely packed with people, talking, laughing, enjoying tea in delicate china cups and saucers alongside plates of all the sweet, culinary delights that this place had to offer.

He saw a hand rise and wave and he spotted Lorna over in one corner and he went over to join her, kissing her on the cheek in greeting. She'd changed out of her work clothes and wore a casual outfit of a moss-green tee shirt under loose denim dungarees. A polka-dotted hairband held her hair back from her face and she wore bright white trainers. She managed to pull off the look effortlessly and he was very impressed.

'You look great.'

In comparison he felt as if he'd not made any effort. He still wore the outfit he'd worn at work. Dark trousers. Shirt. Work shoes. Should he have gone casual too? Jeans and a tee?

'Thank you. Clothes may maketh man, but they certainly camouflage women.'

'Who are you hiding from?'

'Patients. They often don't recognise me if I put my hair up and wear something really casual.'

'Like Clark Kent. Maybe you should add glasses, too?'

She laughed and reached into a bag she had at her side, pulling out a pair of black-framed glasses. 'Way ahead of you.'

He noticed she had a cup of tea in front of her that was now empty. She must have got here early. 'More tea?'

'They take orders at the table here.'

'All right.' He turned to get someone's attention. The girls behind the counter seemed to be whizzing about non-stop, but every now and again they looked up into the store and when they did he raised his hand and got a smile and a nod from a young girl with her hair twisted up into a messy bun.

Emilia—according to her name tag—arrived at their table, notepad and pencil in hand. 'What can I get you?'

'Two pots of tea, please.'

'Anything to eat?'

'What would you recommend?' he asked.

'Today's special is a toffee and honeycomb cheesecake, but my personal recommendation is the limoncello and mascarpone cheesecake if you like something a little zesty.'

Oliver looked at Lorna. 'What do you fancy?'

'Do you have any of that chocolate hazelnut left?'

Emilia nodded. 'One slice.'

'I'll have that, please.'

'And I'll try the limoncello, thank you.'

'Great choice!' Emilia zoomed away to fill their order.

'She seems nice.'

'I think she's Verity's niece.'

'How is Verity doing?'

'I haven't seen her, but she's due a check-in with me in a week or so. Have you heard from Jo recently? I'm assuming she's still in the clear?'

He nodded. 'I don't hear from her often, but when she has a scan, she always emails me to let me know the results. Last time I heard from her everything was good.'

'That's great. I'm pleased for her. You both went through a really difficult time together. I guess that bonds people in ways that good times don't.'

'I guess it does.' His thoughts seemed to take him away and she wanted to pull him back.

'We went through a difficult time together, didn't we? Medical school, I mean. All those tests and assessments. Placements. All those times we worked into the early hours of the morning writing essays, losing sleep, and you had it worse than me. You had Jo to worry about.'

He laughed. 'Yeah. It wasn't a walk in the park. It would have been harder if I'd not had you. You got me through that.'

She shrugged. 'I just helped. You still had to put in the work and you had so much stress going on personally. You always impressed me with how you dealt with it. You were always upbeat. Making jokes.'

'Well, if I didn't laugh, I'd have probably cried.'

Lorna nodded. 'I always envied you, you know.'

'Envied me?'

'Absolutely! You seemed so laid-back about everything. Even with what was going on with Jo, you seemed so relaxed about it all. I wished I had that. I remember being tense a lot.'

'I was just projecting. I wasn't as relaxed as you thought I was. I remember thinking that if I just pretended that I didn't have to be stressed, then maybe I wouldn't be. I was trying to convince myself that everything was all right, when it wasn't. Some of those oncology classes were hard to get through.'

'But you and Jo…you were both very strong.'

'In public, maybe. But at home, in private… life was very tense.'

Emilia brought their pots of tea and two slices of cheesecake on a plate. 'Enjoy!' she said before disappearing quickly again.

'Well, these look great. Want to try a bite of mine?'

'Sure!'

He used his fork to slice a piece of his limoncello and raised the fork to her mouth. He tried not to think too hard of the way her lips opened and she accepted his offering, her lips sliding off the fork to consume the cheesecake.

'Mmm!' she said, her noises of pleasure doing strange things to his insides. 'Oh, my God, you forget how good the food is here. Try mine.' She made a forkful of her chocolate hazelnut and passed the fork over for him to hold.

He tasted the cheesecake, the smoothness, the softness. The bitter kick of the dark chocolate kicked into sweetness with the nutty taste of hazelnut. 'Oh, my God, that's amazing.'

'Isn't it?'

For a while the two of them were quiet whilst they devoured their desserts. But like all good things, they were gone too quickly and they were left to press their forks into the crumbly biscuit bottom to mop up all the crumbs. 'Now, if a plate of these were waiting for me at the end of that marathon we're going to do, then I think I'd get a record time,' Lorna said.

'Maybe we could dangle one at the end of a stick in front of you and you can chase it for twenty-six miles?'

She laughed. 'Sign me up! This is nice. Being here with you.'

He wanted to say the same thing, because it was true. He'd missed this. Sitting at a table with Lorna and spending time with her, only this time instead of there being a pile of textbooks in front of them, they could relax and enjoy the moment. As much as he would allow himself to relax. He didn't want to give her the wrong idea, even if his mind was making him think about her too much. 'So what do you do for fun? When you're not training for a marathon?'

Lorna shrugged. 'I read a lot. I garden. I bake. I've even learned how to sew with a machine and I made myself a pair of curtains for my bedroom. I've become a domestic goddess.'

He smiled at the image of Lorna in an apron, with sunlight streaming in behind her, surrounded by bluebirds and squirrels like some old-fashioned animation. 'That's amazing! But all of that—that's for your home. What do you do that's just *for you*? That broadens your horizons? That amazes you? How do you treat yourself?'

'I don't know. I'm not sure I ever have.'

'You haven't been travelling?'

'I've always been working.'

'You've never thought to take some time off and go and see the world?'

'No, I guess not. For a long time Craig and trying for a baby were my world. After I learned of the affair, healing myself by working was my world. What about you? Have you travelled?'

He nodded. 'I didn't realise how small my

world had become until I'd travelled. I've watched the sun rise over the Great Pyramids of Egypt. I've ridden through a desert on a camel. I watched orangutans in Borneo. Swam with sharks off the coast of Australia. Watched the sunset in Tokyo. Millions of miles, through many, many countries and still all I wanted to do was come home.' He smiled ruefully. 'We're small creatures, with small lives and endless worries and concerns. We do what we can do to survive it.'

'Well, your travels sound amazing and I, for one, am glad you came home. This *is* home now, I take it?'

He made a show of looking around him. At the people at the next tables. Out of the window at Clearbrook village and finally back at the woman sitting opposite. 'It is.'

She beamed. 'Good. I hadn't realised how much I'd missed having you around, you know? We may have just started out as study buddies, but I really came to depend on you and, though I was excited to strike out into the world and try and make it on my own, I'm glad that we've found each other again.'

'Me too.' He'd not really thought too much about what Lorna had got out of their relationship. He'd known and understood what he'd got from it, but what had he given her in return?

Some jokes? Comradeship? Someone else to bounce ideas off? Someone who had the same goals to share space with?

He'd known that she'd liked him, in spite of the fact that he'd been dedicated to Jo and nothing would ever have happened between them. Because he'd also known, deep down inside, that he *could* see himself with her. That he'd often wished that his life had been different and that when Lorna had come into his life, he could have been with her instead. He'd told himself it would be simpler. Easier. A relationship with Lorna would not have had cancer woes and chemo side effects. It would have been normal. And then he'd felt guilty about that.

And now here they were, early fifties, single, living in the same village, both divorced, both having gone through a fertility journey, both still really keen to renew a friendship that they'd started all those years ago.

The question was…how would it finish?

'So you're here for your six-week mother and baby check?' Lorna smiled.

Yasmin Groves was with her baby daughter, Daisy, who was just over six weeks old. Her special baby. A child she'd conceived after a stillbirth. This was the woman who had inspired Lorna to run for a stillbirth charity.

'Yes, that's right.'

'And how do you feel everything's going?'

'Great! Yeah. I could do with more sleep, but I guess every new mum says that, don't they?'

Lorna laughed. 'Most do, yes.'

'I think it's because I'm always up checking on her. We've got a monitor and all of that, but still, with what happened...'

Lorna nodded, understanding completely. 'Okay, let's take a look at you, Mum, first, whilst Daisy is still asleep and then we'll give her a look-over. Is that okay?'

'Yep.'

She glanced at her notes on the computer. 'So, it says here you had a natural delivery with a second-degree tear.'

'Yeah.'

'Any problems going to the toilet?'

'No, not really. It stung to begin with, but that's stopped now.'

'Okay, and are you breastfeeding?'

Yasmin nodded.

'Okay, let's check your blood pressure.' Lorna wrapped the cuff around Yasmin's arm. She'd had a couple of episodes of high blood pressure during her pregnancy, but her reading today was back to normal. 'That all looks good. How are you managing with Daisy? Looking after her okay? Any problems?'

'She has a bit of colic sometimes, but mostly she's really good and doesn't cry much. Except at night.'

'Okay, and are you still bleeding?'

'No, that stopped a couple of days ago.'

'All right, well, I'd like to examine you, if that's okay? Check the stitches have healed well. If you'd like to go behind the curtain, I'll go get a chaperone.' Lorna managed to grab Bella. She explained the situation and Bella came in and introduced herself to Yasmin through the curtain.

'Ready.'

Lorna adjusted the light so that she could check the stitched area in the perineum. Yasmin had healed very well and Lorna couldn't see any reason as to why there might be any future problems. 'Have you abstained from sex since the birth?'

'Absolutely, yes! I haven't let Jase come near me, much to his dismay. Having these things blow up to twice their size hasn't helped.' She indicated her breasts.

'Well, everything looks okay down there and I'm giving you the all-clear for that, but don't feel like you have to have sex until you're ready and, when you do, go gently.'

Yasmin nodded.

'Are you happy for me to check your breasts?'

'Go ahead.'

Because Yasmin was breastfeeding, it was important for Lorna to check that her breasts and nipples were fine. First time breastfeeders could experience some discomfort and if baby wasn't latching correctly, it could sometimes cause damage to that sensitive area. 'Daisy latching on okay?'

'I think so. We did visit a lactation consultant right at the beginning and that helped with positioning.'

'Well, you look great, so why don't you get dressed? Thank you, Bella.'

Bella smiled and said goodbye and slipped from the room.

'Is that the other new doctor?'

'One of them, yes, though they've been here a few weeks now.'

'I met the other one the other day in the village. The guy? He's handsome.'

Lorna didn't want to ask her which one. Both Max and Oliver were handsome. So she simply smiled and waited for Yasmin to come out from behind the curtain before they could assess the baby.

'So, how is Daisy? Sleeping through the night?'

'Sometimes.'

'Feeding okay?'

'Yeah. I was alarmed at how often she was

feeding to begin with, but I think it was a comfort thing, so I got her a dummy, which has been better.'

'Lots of wet nappies?'

'Plenty. And why did no one tell me about the way poo changes colour in the beginning?'

Lorna smiled. 'Excellent. That all sounds normal. Does she follow your face and voice?'

'She seems to.'

'Okay, can you get her undressed for me and I'll perform a physical examination?'

She waited for Yasmin to undress her baby. Daisy wasn't fond of the idea of being undressed and began to cry as she was stripped down to her nappy.

'Oh, it's okay. It's okay.' Lorna picked the baby up and swayed a little with her to reassure her, enjoying the feel of a baby in her arms. These were always the best moments of a mother and baby check for her. When she got to be with the baby and imagine how her own life might have been different if she had fallen pregnant with a child. Would she have been a single mother because of Craig's affair? Or would she still be in a marriage, unaware of her husband's infidelity? Yearning for a child of her own made these moments special, when she could imagine, no matter how briefly, how things might have been.

Daisy gazed at her with wide blue eyes, her little tongue poking out of her mouth as she made a small noise. She was a beautiful baby and Lorna felt a longing ache. A grief for something she had never been given. A grief for something that had been stolen away from her.

All the baby's observations were normal. She had all the right reflexes, her chest and abdomen sounded good. Her umbilicus had healed well and her hips had good flexion and movement. 'She looks great.' Lorna handed Daisy back to her mum and told her she could dress her again. 'Well, I'm happy to sign both of you off as doing brilliantly.'

'Great! These first few weeks have been nerve-racking.'

'That's understandable, considering what you went through. You're booked in to have her first immunisations in two weeks.' Lorna checked her future appointments.

'Thank you.'

She waved Daisy and Yasmin goodbye, watching as Yasmin manoeuvred the pushchair through the doorway and out into the corridor. As she did so, she spotted Oliver saying goodbye to a patient. He stepped back so Yasmin could pass and she watched him look down at the baby and say hello.

Yasmin paused, politely, so Oliver could converse with Daisy in a baby voice and Lorna smiled, watching him. He would have made a good father.

What would their lives have been like if she'd married Oliver rather than Craig? Would they have still struggled with fertility? There was no medical reason why Oliver couldn't have kids and though she'd been diagnosed with a hostile uterus, it might have worked with him.

Maybe together they might have been amazing parents with a couple of kids by now? Maybe even thinking about grandchildren?

As Yasmin left, he turned and caught her gaze, smiling at her. 'She was beautiful. Did you see her?'

Lorna nodded. 'I did.'

And I held her in my arms and ached for all the babies I lost.

She'd also lost him. For a time. Yet now she had him back. Maybe they could be more than they were before? Having him here in Clearbrook brought all of the old feelings back.

Maybe Oliver could bring her happiness?

But she was too old to have babies now. He could still have them if he found someone a little younger. But it hurt to think that she could lose him to another woman.

That she had nothing to offer.

* * *

'You ever think of having kids?' Max asked Oliver.

Having a baby had been an obsession for Jo after her cancer treatment. She'd had her eggs frozen before she began chemotherapy and when she'd decided that she was ready to start trying for a child after it all, she'd been through so much—*they'd* been through so much—that he'd agreed. There had to be something good at the end of all of that.

Oliver had always wanted kids and he'd hoped for them after Jo's treatment was over. He'd always thought he would make a great father. Watching them grow. A little bit of him, maybe seeing his own eyes in someone else's face, noting similar mannerisms in his little miniature self. Wondering if they'd take after him or their mother more. Making them laugh, tickling their tummies, playing with them outdoors or taking them to after-school clubs, watching them become a person of their own and hopefully guiding them towards good life decisions.

There'd been many good days with Jo and he'd clung to those, telling himself that the reason their relationship had always been so strained was because of the cancer. But when the cancer had gone, they could move forwards. What better way to do that than to cement their relationship with a baby?

IVF had been incredibly difficult. It had made their life all about Jo's health, all over again. Just as many tests and scans. Just as much bloodwork. Just as many needles and procedures, it seemed. The ovary hyperstimulation in one cycle had really knocked Jo for six. They'd stopped IVF for a bit to give her chance to recover, even though Jo had not wanted to wait, but Oliver had insisted upon it. For both of them. Of course, Jo had hoped that somehow, miraculously, she would get pregnant naturally in the meantime, even though that had been virtually impossible.

The stress of it all came back to him, every time he got to hold a baby in his arms, or stop to admire one. The drive to procreate, to have a child of their own, a symbol of their love, had been the thing to finally tear them apart. The resulting failure had caused recriminations and bitterness and so, since then, he was very often in awe and felt admiration and a little bit of envy for those who managed it so effortlessly.

But he'd given up on that dream now.

He caught sight of Max's face and realised he must have been daydreaming for a little while. 'Once, but it never worked out that way. What about you? Did you ever think you'd have more than one?'

'Before I met Anna, my wife, I kind of imagined I'd have two, maybe three, but I guess life teaches you to manage your expectations in new and cruel ways sometimes.'

'It certainly does. I was sorry to hear about what happened with your wife.'

Max acknowledged his sympathy with a nod. 'You faced cancer with your wife, too. Jo, wasn't it?'

'Yes.'

'And she's okay now?'

'I suppose. We don't really keep in contact except for Christmas cards, and she'll email me whenever she gets scan results.'

Max nodded. 'And you and Lorna? Friends for ever, I hear?'

Instantly, he smiled at the thought of her. 'Until death do us part.'

Max raised an eyebrow. 'Isn't that usually a vow said in marriage?'

As if summoned, Lorna entered the staffroom at that moment and smiled at them both. 'Hello. Max, did you get my email about Stella's results? They came through to me, rather than you.'

'I did, yes—I've given her a call to come in and see me about them.'

'Great. What a day, huh? I'm ready to go home, put my feet up and relax in front of the television with a bowl of popcorn.'

'No training tonight?' Max asked.

'Rest day,' said Oliver, smiling at Max, but his companion's attention was stolen by the arrival of Bella into the staffroom. Max excused himself and got up to go and talk to her.

Oliver went over to Lorna and nodded at the other two doctors. 'Think something's brewing there?'

Lorna raised an eyebrow. 'Since day one! They can't keep their eyes off one another.'

'Do they know it?'

'I'm not sure.' She gave a small laugh and glanced at him, her eyes twinkling with amusement. 'But they seem a nice couple, don't you think?'

'They have a lot in common.'

'So do we.'

Oliver smiled, but he felt afraid of what it would mean if he began to think of Lorna as a romantic partner. He'd be lying if he said he'd never thought of it. 'But we have decades of history. I'm not sure I'd want to be in the dating pool these days.'

'No? Why not?' She sounded curious. A little hurt.

'It sounds exhausting and I only have enough energy these days for work and practice runs with my marathon partner, who, let's face it, rewards me greatly with a large variety of baked goods.'

Lorna smiled. 'She sounds like a keeper.'

'She is.' And without thinking, he swooped in and dropped a kiss upon her cheek.

When he realised what he'd done, he felt himself colour as Lorna herself was too. He looked around them to make sure no one had noticed, but Max and Bella were too absorbed with one another to notice anything he and Lorna might have done. So he simply smiled. 'I guess I ought to head for home. Still have some boxes to unpack.'

'Need any help?'

'No, it's fine. Besides, you have a date with a bowl of popcorn and I wouldn't want to be the man to get in the way of that.'

'I'm happy to help if you'd like. I'm actually quite nerdy, would you believe? I love sorting and organising.'

He had a flash of memory. Of calling round to her new student digs once. Her old place had been closed due to a mould problem and she'd been assigned a new room. Her door had been propped open by a box, music had been blaring and she'd been arranging furniture and her possessions. Well, that had probably been the intention to begin with. But she'd been standing there, her back to him, not knowing he was there, headphones on, a wire trailing over half the room to a big old stereo and she'd been dancing, one hand on each headphone as if she were absorbed in the music. He'd stood there and watched her move, lost in the music, and he'd been a little hypnotised by the sway of her hips and the soft smile on her face.

She had given him so much and she wanted to help him now, too. Was that so wrong? 'Well, I guess I wouldn't say no to an extra pair of hands, if you really mean it?'

'Sure! I'll go home and change and then come round to yours.'

'I'll cook.'

'Perfect.'

CHAPTER SIX

SHE'D NEVER BEEN in Oliver's house before. She'd seen his student digs briefly once. She'd met him at the door and had only glimpsed inside and seen posters on the wall of some rock band and a messy bed. She could remember good-naturedly teasing him about tidying up, but, to be fair, he'd hardly ever been at his digs. He'd slept there, but not much else. He'd always been round at Jo's.

So knocking on his door this evening, brandishing a tub of apple turnover pastries that she'd baked the day before, made her curious and excited. Would he still be messy? What would his house, his choice of furnishings, his style, tell her about him?

When he opened the door to greet her, the first thing she noticed was that he'd changed into a pair of dark jeans and a black fitted tee. His hair looked damp and he was barefoot. And smelt great! He looked as if he were about to shoot a men's aftershave commercial.

'Hey, come on in.'

'I brought pastries for dessert.' She raised the tub.

'Great.' He stepped back to let her pass, dropping a kiss upon her cheek.

The hallway was dark enough to spare her blushes, but light enough to show the walls painted in a soft, light grey. There were two framed pictures on the walls—a graphite drawing of lions and another of elephants.

Oliver led her to the kitchen, where pots were bubbling away on the stove. It was a modern kitchen with white units and shiny countertops. The small round kitchen table was glass, with a succulent in a pot sitting in the middle. The kitchen screamed minimalism. Everything had its place, she noticed, when he reached into a cupboard and all the bottles, jars and cans inside were perfectly ordered. She was impressed. Not untidy any more...

'I'm cooking lobster linguine. Is that all right?'

'Great! Where did you get lobster from in Clearbrook?'

'I ordered it online.' He laughed. 'Can't go wrong with a bit of lobster tail. Take a seat. Drink?'

'Whatever you're having is fine.'

'I was just about to open a cheeky Sauvignon Blanc, but if you're driving...?'

'I walked here. Wine is fine.'

He opened the slimline wine cabinet and pulled out a bottle, which he opened and poured two glasses, handing her one. 'Thought we'd eat first before tackling those boxes, if that's okay?'

'Sure. How many are there?'

'About ten left over from the move. I've got most of the important stuff out now, so I'm sure this is just stuff from the old attic space, but it's worth going through to see if there's anything I can get rid of or donate.'

She nodded and sipped her wine. It was dry, yet fruity, leaving notes of citrus, tropical fruits and gooseberry. 'Mmm. This is lovely.'

He clinked her glass with his. 'To unpacking memories.'

'Unpacking memories.' She took another sip. 'You really have no idea what's in those boxes?'

'Nope. I just emptied the attic and they'd been in there for years.'

'Well, maybe I should let you open them first. Just in case, you know.'

'In case of what?'

'In case there's anything private or embarrassing in them.'

Oliver turned to look at her. 'Actually, that's a good idea. I did misplace that blow-up doll once...' He smirked.

Lorna smiled. 'Funny. You're a funny guy.'

He laughed and gave the pasta a swirl with a wooden spoon. 'This has got about five minutes. Let me give you the whistle-stop tour of the place.'

Holding her glass, she followed him around. The rest of the cottage was pretty much like the kitchen. Modern. Clean lines. No clutter. Everything perfectly organised. Even the books on his bookshelf had been arranged by colour.

'Who taught you to be so neat?' she asked.

'I taught myself.'

'Not Jo?'

'No. For the majority of our marriage, Jo was either resting in bed or sleeping on a couch. Her treatments made her exhausted and in the years in which she *seemed* well, she never really wanted to waste her precious time alive with simple, boring tasks like cleaning or organising, so I did it. We had enough chaos in our lives with health matters, without the house being a tip, too. The clarity of being in a clean space helped calm my mind when our world was being ripped apart.'

'I get that. When *we* were trying for a baby and going through IVF, it seemed all that mattered were my hormone levels, the thickness of my uterine lining, my blood results and whether that damned test would be positive or not. Everything else would fall by the wayside. We tried to be disciplined. Look after ourselves. Eat well. Keep the house right. But we were both working and busy and tired when we got home… I remember saying clearly that I wished we had a cleaner. Maybe I should have hired you?' she said with a smile as he led her up the stairs towards the bedrooms.

There were two bedrooms in this cottage. One was a small box room. Oliver had a desk in there, with a computer and a chair and a small bookcase with a pot plant on it. Then he led her to his bedroom. She stood in the doorway and looked around.

'We'd have had a lot to talk about if we'd known each other whilst we were each married, don't you think?'

'Heck, yeah.' She imagined what it would have been like to have sat down at night and shared her pain over IVF with Oliver. He would have got it. He would have understood. Craig had been there for her, of course he had, but, with hindsight now, she could sense that he'd been distracted. As if he'd been one step removed from all that had been going on, which he had been because he'd always been in another room texting his girlfriend. She'd thought he'd stayed up late at night, after she'd gone to bed, because the stress of the IVF had made it so he couldn't sleep, but he'd really been having late-night conversations with another woman he'd been trying to keep sweet.

If Oliver had been there, if he'd known Craig, would he have liked him? Would he have noticed that something was awry with their relationship? Would he have tried to warn her? Or had a quiet chat with Craig, man to man? She liked the idea of him trying to protect her.

Oliver's bedroom was neat and uncluttered like the rest of the cottage. He had a double bed, with a soft, white duvet and cushions and a counterpane in a soft cream. A book sat on his nightstand, next to an alarm clock. There was a fluffy rug on the floor and stacked up against one wall were the last few boxes that she was here to help with.

'This is nice,' she said, trying not to imagine Oliver lying in the bed, half naked, with beckoning eyes. It was an image that was difficult to get out of her head.

'Thanks.' He glanced at his watch. 'Better get back to that lobster tail. We don't want to overcook it.'

No. That would be bad. Just as bad as imagining your best friend naked. She forcibly pushed the image from her mind and followed him down the stairs, trying not to notice the trimness of his waist, or the way the jeans moulded to his body. She knew he had good legs. She'd seen them when they'd gone on their training runs. He had great thighs. Strong. Powerful. Covered in a fine smattering of dark hair. Nothing too thick. He didn't look like a werewolf or anything.

As they reached the kitchen, he poked the lobster and declared it ready to serve.

They sat in the lounge to eat their lobster linguine. There was a film on the television that played low in the background as they chatted about their day and once Oliver had refilled their wine, they headed back upstairs to tackle the boxes.

'Okay, let's get this done.'

They'd brought up some bin bags and a few spare boxes—one labelled 'Recycle', one labelled 'Keep', another labelled 'Charity Shop'.

'Should we work on one box together or do one each?' she asked.

'One each? Might work quicker?' he suggested.

'Okay.' She pulled a box towards her. There was nothing written on the outside and the tape that held it together was so old, it tore off easily. Opening it up, she found a box of paper and card, with some stamps and ribbons inside.

'Ah, Jo's card-making phase,' Oliver said. 'She wanted something to do when she had no energy to go out and she thought it would save us money if she made her own. It didn't.' He smiled.

'Charity shop?'

He nodded.

She emptied all the things from the old box into the new one and then reached for another box. This one had writing on the side. It simply said 'uni'. Intrigued, she opened it up as Oliver worked his way through a box of books.

The box had a couple of old textbooks in it. Medical texts, obviously, but there was a photo album in there, too. She opened it up and smiled.

There were photos of the two of them from when they'd been friends before. It felt strange to be looking back at their youth. Oliver with no silver in his hair and no glasses. Her hiding in a big grey sweatshirt, holding an A4 folder to her chest as Oliver pulled a funny face behind her, his two fingers making bunny ears behind her head.

'What's so funny?' Oliver asked.

'Us. Look.' She turned the album round so he could see.

'Wow.'

There were pictures of their other classmates. Pictures taken in lecture theatres, labs. One of them all dressed in white coats and face masks. There was even a series of pictures from that time they'd done Halloween together and they'd all dressed up as zombie doctors and nurses and covered themselves in prosthetics and fake blood. She remembered that night. Lorna had actually fallen over and cut her knee for real and Oliver had used saline from the IV drip he'd been pushing around to clean it and then ripped more of his torn shirt to mop up the real blood and make sure she was okay.

'I remember thinking how you'd be a good doctor, even then. You had an amazing bedside manner.' The fact that they were now sitting beside his bed was not lost on her.

She turned more pages, got lost in even more memories and when the photos ran out, she noticed that there were other items in the slots where the photos ought to sit. A cinema stub ticket. A dried yellow flower. Odd. She looked at the stub. Realised it was for a film that she'd seen at the cinema with Oliver. A comedy to cheer him up.

But the flower?

'What was this?' she asked softly, touched that he had kept the cinema ticket stub.

Oliver looked over and smiled. 'You don't remember?'

She shook her head.

'It had been a really hot day. It was lunchtime. You'd been sitting out on the grass absorbing a few rays. You made a daisy chain as we were talking and I asked you if you could do one with buttercups. You said buttercups were for seeing if you loved butter and you plucked it from the grass and held it under my neck. Said I did and then passed me the flower.'

'And you kept it?' That was sweet.

'Of course. You gave it to me.' He looked away awkwardly. A little embarrassed.

He'd kept the buttercup. The cinema stub. The pictures in the album were of them. A few others, too, but mostly them. Oliver had cherished these items. They'd meant something to him.

'Keep?' she asked, feeling emotional at the thought of how he had kept the little things. To hold onto the memories that they'd had together.

'Keep.' He stared back at her. And for a moment they were both lost in *what-might-have-been*.

She felt a heat bloom begin in the centre of her chest and her first thought was, *Great, what a brilliant moment to experience a hot flush*, but it didn't rise up her neck and into her face the way her usual hot flushes did. This one sat in the centre of her chest and slowly worked its way *down*, making her aware of her entire body. An arousal, as her whole body became alive with anticipation.

She'd not wanted anybody physically for a long, long time. With Craig, sex had become something that was supposed to be functional but that didn't work. In the end, it had felt like something she ought to do. A responsibility to keep connected with her husband. Any conception had been going to take place in a lab and after each implantation they wouldn't sleep together, just in case. In the end, they'd got used to not sleeping with one another at all. So she'd stopped thinking of herself as a sexual being and then, after realising the betrayal, she'd been glad they hadn't been intimate for a long time.

But here it was. Those stirrings of lust and desire that she'd thought long gone. Not dormant at all, but alive, well and raging. For Oliver.

And he was looking at her in a way that made her think that perhaps he felt the same. They'd both had physicality removed from their relationships and to experience it again, to be aware, to want, to need, to *yearn* for touch, was a delicious sensation. And to experience it with Oliver was indescribable and as their fingers brushed as she passed him the pressed flower, they maintained the connection. As if neither of them wanted to part, as if the electricity that was racing up and down her arm was also racing around him and, together, they made a circuit. Apart, separate, they were nothing, but touching? Connected? They came alive! Fizzing and sparking and the intensity of it was so powerful!

He cleared his throat and looked away. Pulled his hand back. Clearly uncomfortable.

She was upset that she felt this way for her best friend in the whole world and yet, clearly, he did not feel the same way. She'd thought they'd had a moment over the buttercup. She'd thought they'd connected, shared a mutual recognition of desire, because she'd thought she'd seen something in his gaze, too. But he had pulled away. Now he was getting to his feet, suggesting he ought to fetch more wine as their glasses were empty.

When he'd gone downstairs, she let out a breath and ran her hands through her hair. Maybe it was for the best? Because what if, after all this time, they were incompatible as partners? Maybe all they were destined to be was good friends and nothing more?

If I got together with him, he'd not be able to have children ever. And maybe I just imagined that moment? Seeing and feeling what I wanted to see? What I wanted him to be feeling?

She could not take the chance for him to have kids away from him. He deserved happiness. He deserved to find it and start a family, whilst he still had time and energy.

Reverently, she placed the album into the Keep box, broke down the old one so that it laid flat, ready for the recycling bin. She moved on to another box.

You can't lose your friend.

* * *

Downstairs in the kitchen, Oliver splashed cold water onto his face, then stood for a moment, bent over the sink, trying to rein in his feelings.

He'd forgotten about that photo album. About the cinema stub and the buttercup. Why had he kept that flower? It was just a buttercup! Hardly a rose or anything, a true flower of romance. Most people would consider a buttercup a weed. But he'd kept it, because in that moment back then, when Lorna had leaned in towards him, smiling, holding that flower next to his throat, he had felt something so strongly for her that he'd almost had to hold his breath. How she'd met his gaze, laughed and said, 'You *love* butter.' And she'd handed it to him, before glancing at her watch and running off to catch her next lecture, completely unaware of how much that moment had mattered to him. Those were the sorts of moments he'd wanted with Jo and to be having them with someone else had made him feel so…

That very same morning, he'd had a row with Jo. She'd accused him of spending too much time with Lorna. She'd yelled that he'd rather spend time with his classmate than he would with her, his girlfriend. He'd known it was insecurity and he'd felt guilty that he'd caused her that. Jo had been struggling since the diagnosis of her breast cancer at such an early age, knowing she would have to have a mastectomy. She'd struggled with her idea of losing herself as a woman. He'd tried so hard to be supportive, but it had been difficult.

It had absolutely not been true that a mastectomy would make her any less of a woman. A woman was more than a pair of breasts. He'd not cared whether she'd had them or not—what he'd truly wanted was for her to be happy and healthy. It had been her character and her ability to make him laugh that had made him view Jo as a girlfriend. And they'd been together so long at that point.

But he'd begun to feel so alone. Jo had been down for months. He hadn't been able to touch her without her saying that he was pressuring her and, sure, it had probably been wrong for him to have felt something as Lorna had leant in with that buttercup, laughter in her eyes, but he hadn't been able to help it. The cancer had made him feel trapped. He'd been trying to be honourable and gentlemanly by supporting Jo no matter what, but their moments together had been swathed in test results and tumour markers and they hadn't been getting time to make happy memories and so when Lorna had leaned in like that...

It was a happy memory and, selfishly, he'd wanted to keep it.

He'd felt relief when she'd run off to a lecture, leaving him sitting there on that grass holding a buttercup. He'd wanted to remember the way Lorna had made him feel alive and he'd pressed the flower into a textbook, knowing he'd wanted to keep that moment for when things got tough.

It had been vanity. Seeing Lorna uncover it just now and the way she'd looked into his eyes after? He'd felt a surge of hormones, felt a need for Lorna in a way he'd been trying to control for some time now...

Oliver had played enough games. He'd been on an emotional roller coaster for too many years, way longer than he ought to have been. It was a ride he should have got off years ago. He didn't want to play games with Lorna.

Because he wasn't sure if he would win.

Or lose.

So, he would just have to remain her friend.

They were walking her home. Oliver had said it was the least he could do after she'd helped him finish unpacking those last few boxes.

They walked in a companionable silence through Clearbrook and Lorna's mind was filled with all that she had learned. She'd thought she was the one with hidden feelings for Oliver when they were younger. She'd thought that he had only ever seen her as a study partner and then a good friend. A best friend.

But what if she'd been wrong? What if Oliver had seen her as more than that?

Had he felt trapped in his relationship with Jo? She knew they'd had a few sticky moments, but she'd put that down to the stress of their situation. Cancer was a lot to grapple with at such a young age.

Her mind was awhirl with thoughts and unanswered questions. 'Can I ask you something?'

Oliver looked at her. Smiled. 'Sure. What's up?'

'It's about when we were at med school.'

He sucked in a breath. 'Okay.'

'Did you ever…?' She let out a small laugh, unable to believe that she was actually going to be brave enough to ask this question. 'Did you ever wonder what your life might have been like if you'd *not* been with Jo?'

He nodded. 'Of course. I think everybody at some point thinks about the road they didn't take. Or about how, if they went back in time, they'd make different choices with the benefit of hindsight. Why? What would you have changed?'

'Wow. Okay. Well, sometimes I think that… I wished I had been braver and spoken up more.'

'Okay.'

'That I would have been more aware of what Craig was up to and confronted him about it earlier instead of going through that whole pantomime.'

A pause. 'Oh.'

'Sometimes, I feel like I've been much too passive in life. Letting other people make my big decisions. So…yeah, I'd change that.' She laughed nervously, her face red and hot. 'Be more assertive.'

'I've thought about what it would have been like if we'd known each other when we were both facing the struggles that we did in trying to have our own families.'

'Oh. You have?' Now she truly didn't know what to say. She'd thought of this so often. She'd felt jealous of Jo having Oliver by her side as she'd been going through it. And she'd not felt proud of herself for having that emotion, or for thinking less of Craig at the time, because her own husband had been there for her physically at each appointment. He'd listened to her when she'd cried. Soothed her when she'd been sad. But had she truly felt that he'd been by her side one hundred per cent? No, she hadn't.

Especially in that last IVF cycle. That was the cycle where everything had slowly begun to fall apart and she'd felt his distance; she'd lain on those examining beds alone. Craig had sat on the opposite side of his room, tapping away at his phone. Had he been texting his mistress even then? He'd always denied it, but why should she believe him? He'd lied to her in the most terrible way possible.

'Do you ever think about...' she paused to take in a deep breath '...what it might have been like if we—?' She wasn't brave enough to finish her own sentence. She blushed madly. But then she thought about what she'd just said, about wishing she'd been braver, and she just blurted it out. 'If we had become a thing?'

Oliver sighed and looked down, formulating an answer.

His reaction made her nervous. As if he was trying to work out how to let her down gently and instantly she felt bad. She should never have asked. Never have shared.

'I think the best thing back then was for us to remain friends more than anything else. Don't get me wrong, Lorna, I did think about it. Of course I did! Every day that I saw you I had the feelings, but... I think it's best that we remained friends back then and I think it's best that we remain friends now, because I don't want to lose you again. I lost you for over half my life and, now that we're together again, I don't want to risk trying something that might make me lose you.'

Lorna stared back at him, feeling tears burn in her eyes at his words.

She simply nodded and said, 'Maybe you're right.'

CHAPTER SEVEN

THE NEXT MORNING, Lorna had a couple come into her surgery to see her together. Pauline and Avery Goodman were both in their nineties and were both struggling with getting rid of a cough.

She welcomed them both in. Avery walked slowly with a stick and his wife held onto his arm as they both ambled in.

'Please take a seat. It says here on your call note that you're both struggling with a cough, is that right?'

'Yes.' Pauline nodded as they both sank into chairs opposite. 'It won't go away. Avery seems worse than me. He coughs a lot at night and so neither of us are sleeping very well.'

'What sort of cough is it? Dry? Chesty? Are you producing any phlegm?'

'Sort of chesty, we think. Neither of us has sore throats, but we think it started as a cold, but the cough just won't go away.'

'Okay. Well, I'll do some observations and

listen to both your chests and we'll decide on a treatment plan from there, is that okay?'

'Of course, Doctor.'

Lorna began her examination of Pauline first. Her blood pressure was a little high, but nothing too concerning. Probably due to the doctor's visit and the walk in from the waiting room, and clearly she was concerned and stressed about her husband. Her chest actually sounded clear and she had no temperature either, so Lorna wasn't too worried about her.

Her husband, Avery, was a different story.

He had a low fever, his chest rattled, and he was clearly struggling to breathe. What he needed more than anything was a chest X-ray.

'I want to refer you for a chest X-ray, Mr Goodman. What with your fever and your breathlessness, I think you need to be looked at in hospital.'

'Oh, dear,' he managed.

'If it's all right with you, I'm going to call the hospital right now.'

Avery nodded, but clearly he was weary even from just speaking. He had no history of asthma, so that was good, but it was a worrying sight to see him breathing so badly. They shouldn't have left it so long to come in.

She messaged Reception and asked them to order her an ambulance to take Avery in. Normally, she would have asked Pauline and Avery to make their way in to hospital on their own, but Avery's breathing was so strained, Lorna wanted him to be with the right people en route in case things suddenly took a turn for the worse. His heart and his lungs were struggling to do their job and, at his advanced age, it was a huge worry.

'Will he have to stay in, Doctor?' Pauline asked.

'Possibly, yes.'

'Oh. We've never been apart. Not in seventy years.'

'I understand. But it's for the best if you want to see Avery up and about as normal.'

When she went out to ask a receptionist to call the ambulance, Oliver was at Reception.

'Need help?' he asked. 'I've had a no-show. I'm free to assist.'

'That'd be great, thanks.'

Whilst they waited for the ambulance to arrive, Lorna set Avery up with some oxygen as his oxygen saturation score was at eighty-eight. A healthy oxygen level was ninety-four and above. The oxygen brought his levels up a couple of points, but still not enough into healthy levels. Oliver made Pauline a cup of tea to steady her nerves as they waited, keeping her chatting and reassured about her husband, and when the

paramedics arrived—two lovely young men—
the paramedics loaded Avery into their truck and
helped Pauline into the chair beside him.

She was so grateful for Oliver's assistance.

'Good luck,' they both said as the ambulance
doors closed and the vehicle drove away.

Lorna stood there for a moment. 'What must
it be like to have been with the love of your life
for seventy years and to have never been apart?'

'I don't know. Makes you wonder, doesn't it?'
Oliver turned to look at her. 'To have known
someone for that long. To have been able to love
them for so long.'

She stared back at him and nodded.

It made her ache for what she had lost.

Last night, after walking home from Oliver's,
she had felt awkward. They'd had a lovely evening, and then, walking through the village with
the scent of lavender in the air, gazing at people's
wonderful gardens overflowing with blooms and
colour, Oliver at her side, she'd begun to think
that that was the very definition of happiness.
That everything in her world was rosy. Until
she'd stupidly told him that she'd thought about
them being together. Or, at the very least, had
asked him if he'd ever thought about it.

Her hopes had been high. That maybe he
would say the words she so longed to hear. That
maybe he would reach out for her hand and hold

it in his. That maybe, just maybe, he would turn her to face him and kiss her!

But it hadn't happened that way. Oliver was too concerned about their friendship. About not wanting to ruin it if a relationship between them didn't work out, and she understood that. But still, it hurt.

Because she'd begun to have dreams. Dreams of the two of them sharing a life together. And he'd blown that idea out of the water.

He wasn't prepared to risk it.

She wasn't worth the risk.

And she'd been so sad, so upset, that she'd hurried indoors and cried afterwards. She'd lain in bed all night, staring at the ceiling, until exhaustion had snatched her into the realms of disturbing dreams. She'd woken this morning with the determination to give herself some distance from Oliver—personally, at least. To keep him firmly in the work-colleague zone. The friend zone.

As she walked back into Clearbrook Medical Practice with him, she felt so aware of their hands so close together. She could reach out and touch him. Entwine their fingers. A little gesture of togetherness. As if she felt the same things as him. But she couldn't bring herself to do so. What if he rejected her? What if he pulled away, as he had when they'd been sorting boxes? She headed straight for her room.

A rap of knuckles at the door made her heart sink. 'Yes?'

Oliver opened the door. 'May I come in?'

She nodded, but busied herself with signing a couple of prescriptions she'd printed out for patients to collect later.

'Are we okay?'

'Of course!'

'Only, after last night…'

He sounded concerned, but she didn't need him to be.

'I'm fine, Oliver. Honestly.'

'And we're still on for our training run this evening?'

The training run? Damn. She'd forgotten about that. 'Oh, right. Actually, I won't be able to make that. Something's come up.' She hated lying, but she wasn't sure she could handle a run with him tonight, knowing that he'd permanently friend-zoned *her*.

'Really? You're not avoiding me because of last night?'

She looked up at him. Put down her pen. 'Nothing happened last night.' And that was the problem. Because she'd been hoping that it might. 'And I really do have something to do.

We can run tomorrow, okay? Missing one training session won't hurt.'

He nodded. 'Okay. Because the whole thing about making that decision was that I got to keep you as my friend. So that we didn't endanger that. We haven't, have we?'

She forced a smile. 'No, we haven't. I'm still your friend.'

He seemed to believe her.

Lorna was shocked that she could lie to him so well. So believably. Or maybe it wasn't so strange. Hadn't she hidden her true feelings for him before, all those years ago?

'Good. Good. Well, you're still happy for me to bring you morning tea at break time?'

'Absolutely!' Another sweet—yet false— smile. It wasn't okay. It wasn't okay at all! But it was fifteen minutes at most. She could get through that, right?

'Great. Well… I'll see you later, then.'

The next day he decided to make an extra effort with her morning tea, because he felt guilty. Instead of just grabbing two mugs and carrying them through, he cleaned a tray and made a pot of tea. Organised a plate of biscuits and carried it down the corridor and knocked on her door, as he always did at morning breaktime.

'Come in!'

He pushed the door open with a smile, determined to be bright and bubbly. Determined to be his usual self when he was with her. Determined to enjoy their few minutes together, before the rest of the morning beckoned. He had a couple of patients left on his list, then his clinic finished earlier than the other doctors', because today he had an hour of admin scheduled for the morning, before he had to do a house visit.

'Here you go. This is for you.' He passed her a mug of tea. 'And these.' He passed over the plate of biscuits as well.

'Spoiling me.'

'I try.' He'd brought some fruit shortcake biscuits. Knowing that she favoured these over the plain ones in the staffroom.

He was still puzzling over the night before last. Running through her reaction to him saying he wanted to remain friends. It was clear that maybe she'd been hoping for another response and he got that. He understood that. He'd thought about it too.

But he'd already been through so much. Had already been in a relationship that had gone sour and it had been awful. He didn't want that for them. She was his North Star. She brightened his world. He didn't want to ruin that feeling because a little bit of lust or misplaced emotions told him to scratch that itch he so badly wanted to take care of. But a marriage that he'd thought would be for life had ended and he'd got that wrong—how could he be sure about anything any more?

He'd made a bad choice before and he didn't want to make a bad one now. Not this late in life. And he'd grown accustomed to being single. Had thrived in the freedom of it all and he wanted his remaining thirty or forty years of life to be the same. Right?

'So where are we running tonight?'

'Erm, I've worked out a route that takes us all around the outskirts of the village, around the borders of the lavender fields. We pass that castle that's in ruins, go past Eyersham Hall and then back down into Clearbrook.'

'Eyersham Hall? What's that?'

'It's a stately home. Used to belong to some lord. We'll skirt the edge of the property, but it's pretty nice up there.' She sipped at her tea.

He appreciated that she was talking to him as she normally did. Even if her tone sounded a little off. 'Not long until the big race. Think we'll do all right?'

She shrugged. 'I don't know. I guess we ought to talk race strategy. Your pace is sometimes faster than mine, so if you want to run ahead to forge your own time, don't feel like you have to hang back with me.'

He didn't like the sound of that. 'We *start* together, we'll *end* together. I want to cross that finishing line with you.'

Lorna gazed at him briefly, then looked away. 'You're sure we're okay?'

'We're fine.'

The next few days were pretty grim for Lorna. She felt as if she were moving through life in black and white. That she couldn't feel the joy that she usually felt. If a patient had come into her consulting room and said the same thing, she would probably diagnose depression, but she refused to believe it of herself.

She was an optimist. She always looked on the bright side and she tried to do that. Tried to find the joy. It wasn't as if Oliver had left—he was right there. Often in the next room. And she felt the creeping pain and hurt of discovering that the only thing they'd be with one another was friends. And she had to accept that. You couldn't make someone be with you, no matter how much you wanted it.

Colour began to return. She could smile again and when she really sat down and thought about it, she accepted that her friendship with Oliver was eternal. He was here and she was glad that he was and she began to enjoy her time spent with him once again.

Looking back, she could tell it was a grief process she'd had to go through. Grieving the idea of them being together. It was never going to happen, despite the way she still caught him glancing at her when he thought she wasn't looking. The way he'd smile at her, as if he truly loved her.

Those were good things, right? Because having Oliver as her very best friend in the whole world, right by her side, whenever she needed him, was like the next best thing. They continued working together. Running together. He continued to push her to run the next hill, even when she wanted to stop. He was there when, on one run, she tripped on a tree root. She smacked into the floor and winded herself, her knee ringing with initial pain. He got her to sit with her back to the tree trunk and examined her leg.

'What if I've damaged my knee and can't do the marathon? After all this training?' She began to cry, unexpectedly.

'You're going to be fine.'

He palpated the knee, washed it with water from his bottle and pulled off his own tee shirt to mop at the blood oozing from her capillaries.

Honestly, she wasn't bleeding that much, but she very much appreciated the view. Oliver had a nicely toned body. He didn't have a rippling six-pack, he didn't have pecs you could bounce an apple off, but he was handsomely muscled just enough for it to be seen.

He dabbed at her wound until she stopped oozing and got her to straighten and bend her leg to make sure nothing was broken.

It wasn't. But it still hurt, as did her palms from where she'd hit the dirt. Oliver helped her to her feet after a period of rest and draped her arm around his shoulder to support her, until she felt able to walk without assistance.

He helped her forge on when she was sore and in pain, knowing that in the marathon she would hit a wall, both physically and emotionally, and she needed to know how to push on through. He brought her tea on their morning breaks, and the way he refused to give up on her when she was struggling in those early days meant the world to her.

He had her back.

He did love her.

He would always be by her side.

She signed them up for a competitive ten-kilometre race, in which there'd be hundreds of runners. It was a cross-country race and she thought it would be good practice for them to run with lots of other people.

They lined up at the starting line with over one hundred others and set off at a good pace when the whistle went.

It had been just over a week since the knee incident and she was feeling good, despite there being some bruising to it. It felt different to be running with others. The atmosphere of the race, the crowd cheering them on, actually made them run faster than their usual pace and they finished the race together, Oliver holding her hand raised high as they crossed the finish line in an excellent time of one hour and twenty-one minutes.

A marshal draped medals over their necks and it felt so good! The marathon itself was getting closer and closer and they were both feeling good about it.

Lorna still had *thoughts* about Oliver. *Emotions.* She loved him. She would always love him. But each time her heart decided to run away with all these fantasies about them being together, she would very firmly remind herself that they were just friends and fantasies were just that. A little bit of escapism. What mattered was that she was with him every single day and that they could laugh together and work together and that it was comfortable and good between them.

She'd not liked it when she'd felt a chasm developing between them and she refused to let one develop again. And though she'd vowed to put a distance between them, for the sake of her own sanity, she had tried and yet it had not worked. It had been impossible for her to achieve and, as she'd tried, she'd realised she did not want to achieve it.

Instead, she chose to look forward to work every day because he would be there. She chose to look forward to every evening because they'd be out on a training run or, if it was raining heavily, they'd sit in Oliver's house or her house, study the marathon route and talk strategy. Sometimes they'd order pizza and watch a movie. And at the end of every day, Oliver would kiss her goodnight.

A peck on the cheek. And that moment, every single time that he leant in to drop a kiss onto her cheek, she would close her eyes and soak up every precious moment.

Priti popped her head into his consulting room. 'Got a minute?'

'Sure. But just a minute. I'm about to pop out to do a house call,' Oliver said.

'That's exactly what I wanted to talk to you about.'

'Okay. What's up?'

'Melanie Brooker. Your patient. She was booked in by the trainee we have on Reception, so she didn't know Melanie's reputation, but Miss Brooker has a habit of trying to make complaints against staff. She's not meant to be put with male members of staff because of it, because she always makes allegations of impropriety afterwards. There is a red flag on her record, but our new trainee didn't know to look for it.'

'I see.' Oliver had to admit, he'd not collected Miss Brooker's patient summary yet, let alone had a chance to read it. Whenever a doctor was requested to make a house visit, the practice would print out a patient summary detailing that patient's medications, their most recent history and any other pertinent information, so that the doctor might have some idea of what they were facing when they visited. 'But I'm on call today, so it is my duty to attend.'

'I know. And I'd go with you as a chaperone, but I've got a patient coming in and I can't re-schedule. Might be worth seeing if Bella, Carrie or Lorna is free to go with you. Our nurse has already finished and gone home for the day.'

'I'll send a screen message. See who's free.'

'Great. Document everything, just to cover yourself.'

'Will do.'

It was a problem that could sometimes be faced as a doctor. You were there to help, the patient *needed* help usually, though sometimes the symptoms were bogus, but then they would attack the doctor with accusations afterwards. Sometimes, it could be a loneliness thing, or a mental health thing. It was annoying if the health complaint was a ruse, because that patient was taking up precious time that someone who really needed help could have used instead. The important thing to remember was that the patient still needed help, no matter what, and the only thing to do was be a consummate professional.

Oliver bent over his computer and typed a message that would appear on his colleagues' screens, asking if anyone was free to chaperone. The next thing he knew, Lorna had rapped her knuckles on his door and come in. 'I can come with you. Melanie and I rub along okay, so I can fill you in on the way.'

'Okay, great, thanks.' He sent another message to Bella and Carrie letting them know he had someone and then they grabbed their things and left in Oliver's car. Melanie lived on the outskirts of the village, just past the lavender farm, so they had about a ten-minute drive. It was a lovely day and they would have loved to have walked, but their lunch break was short and they still had afternoon clinics to get through.

'You need to take a left up here and then her house is a right turn on the crest of this hill.'

'Okay.' He pulled into Melanie's driveway. The house looked old, the garden unkempt and overgrown.

'Melanie was an only child, raised by two parents who were both unwell themselves. Her father had a history of back surgeries and lived his final years in a wheelchair. Her mother suffered with agoraphobia and never left the house and therefore Melanie had had to do everything for her parents.'

'Sounds like she never really had a childhood.'

'Not really, no. She missed a lot of school. She never really had a life of her own. When her parents passed, Melanie became a frequent flyer at the surgery. She was lonely. She had no friends and no one to talk to, so she would make up ailments just so she could see somebody. Most weeks, she was seen three or four times and was abusive to the reception team if they didn't give her an immediate appointment. Then the complaints began. We got the sense that complaining gave her an opportunity to feel important, and it also got her into mediation and meetings with the staff.

'Priti wanted to remove Melanie from the doctors' surgery and make her register somewhere else, but Melanie actually suffered a real-life medical emergency after falling down her stairs and broke her back. Like her father she ended up in a wheelchair, and like her mother she developed agoraphobia, so she began to require home visits. Priti agreed to keep her on the roll on the condition that Melanie could not ask for more than one appointment a week, which Melanie reluctantly agreed to.'

'Wow. That's a lot to unpack.' It was a tragic backstory and he had sympathy.

Knocking at the door, they waited for it to be opened and when it did, they smiled a greeting at Melanie.

'Come on in,' she grumbled, before turning her chair and leading the way to a darkened front room.

The house was quite dark. None of the curtains were open and it smelt a bit musty. Oliver wondered when she'd last opened a window. But this lack of care was typical of someone suffering from Melanie's list of complaints.

'Melanie, this is Dr Clandon. He's one of the new doctors that we have at Clearbrook. I don't think the two of you have met yet.'

Oliver felt Melanie look him up and down. 'No. We haven't.'

'It's very nice to meet you, Miss Brooker. How can we help you today?' Her hair wasn't combed. Her clothes were dirty and looked as if she'd been sleeping in them. He knew from the patient summary that Melanie had been given medication for depression.

'I'm not feeling great.'

'I'm sorry to hear that. Can you tell me a little more about not feeling great? Is it something physical? Or is it to do with your mood?'

Melanie shrugged. 'Both, I guess.'

'Okay, and how long have you been feeling a little different?'

'A few weeks. Those pills they gave me don't make no difference.'

'The antidepressants?'

Melanie nodded.

'All right. Sometimes it can take a little while to find the right antidepressant medication that works for you. Something we give commonly can work very well for lots of people, but it doesn't always mean it will be right for you, so it can be trial and error. Are you taking them regularly? It says in your history that you're to take one every day—are you doing that?'

'No. I just take 'em when I feel down, but nothing happens.'

He nodded. 'It can take a while for them to get into your system, but you must take them regularly every day, usually at the same time, or they just won't help you. Is there a reason you're not taking them every day?'

She shrugged. 'I forget. My memory ain't so good.'

'I understand.' He looked around the room, looking for clues that might help him, and couldn't help but spot a smart speaker perched on top of the television. He pointed at it. 'Maybe we could use this to remind you? Set up a repeating reminder alert so that it tells you every day to take your medication.'

'It can do that?'

'Absolutely.'

'All right.'

Oliver set up the reminder for her there and then, so that she would be reminded to take her medication every night at eight o'clock. 'Do you have any physical aches and pains?'

'Not really.'

He'd noticed on the summary that Melanie was also registered as having type two diabetes. 'Are you having your eyes and feet checked regularly? Do they send someone out?'

'I had me eyes tested the other week.'

'And your feet? Do you see a chiropodist? Or podiatrist?'

'No. Never have.'

Melanie was wearing socks, but, like the rest of her clothing, they looked grubby. As if they'd not been changed for weeks.

'Would you allow me to examine you? Perform a set of observations and give your feet a check?'

'All right. But I'm ticklish, mind.'

He smiled. 'I'll be gentle.'

Lorna engaged Melanie in conversation

whilst he quietly performed a set of obs on her. They were talking about mundane matters— the weather, the tourists, if Melanie had heard from her aunt Brenda recently and if she was okay. Lorna kept Melanie engaged and focused on her. They only stopped talking when Oliver had to conduct a blood pressure test.

'Everything's looking good, Melanie. If you're agreeable, I'd like to take a set of basic bloods from you. We've not had a blood test for three years and I'd just like to check that everything's okay.'

'I don't like needles.'

'I can hold your hand, if you'd like?' Lorna suggested. 'Help you focus on something else.'

Melanie grudgingly nodded.

Oliver was so impressed with how Lorna was keeping Melanie calm. There was a framed picture on the television of a black Labrador and Lorna asked her about it. It turned out to be a dog she used to have that had died a couple of years ago.

'Two years ago?' Lorna clarified.

'Yeah.'

That was when the complaints had started. Maybe Melanie was grief-stricken?

'Have you ever thought about getting another dog?' Oliver asked, genuinely curious.

''Course I have. But because of the agoraphobia, I can't get out to the kennels or rescue places to have a look and I'm not sure I'd pass the home visit anyways.'

Oliver had got his blood sample and he sat back on his haunches and considered her. 'What if we could help arrange for someone—a charity maybe—to come and help you sort out the house and make the garden safe? Then you could pass a home visit and maybe get yourself a little dog to keep you company? Perhaps an older pooch that just wants to live its golden years out in relative peace and quiet?'

It was the first time he saw Melanie smile.

A real smile.

One that lit up her eyes.

'I'd like that.'

Oliver smiled back. 'When we get back to the practice, I'll make some calls. Are you happy for me to give your contact details out, so people can call you?'

'I'm not good talking to strangers.'

'Then how about we liaise for you? Act as intermediaries? Then we could call you and let you know what's happening,' Lorna suggested.

'All right. You really think I could get meself another dog?' Melanie looked hopeful.

'We do.' Lorna smiled at Oliver and he smiled back.

'I just need to check your feet.'

Melanie nodded.

He pulled off her grubby socks. Her toenails were overgrown and needed cutting and she looked as though she had a bit of a fungal nail problem, but, thankfully, there were no wounds or damage to the feet that caused immediate concern. 'I'm going to arrange a house visit for a podiatrist, if that's okay? These nails need trimming, because if they curl much more, they're going to go into your foot and, with your diabetes, that could cause a problem for infection. Are you happy for me to arrange that?'

Melanie nodded. 'You two are nice.'

Oliver grinned. 'Thank you. Well, we're going to have to leave now and get back for our afternoon clinics, but I'll ring you later when I've spoken to a few people about helping you out. I'll keep you updated.'

'Thank you.'

'You're very welcome. You take care of yourself and we'll speak soon.'

Back in the car, as they drove away, Lorna let out a huge sigh.

'Did you notice how she opened up when we asked about the dog? I think grief and loneliness have really contributed to her problems, but I feel that we might have helped her today. Steered her towards a bit of optimism. What do you think?'

'Me too. If we can find someone to help her with the house and she can get herself another dog and she looks after it well enough, I think she'll feel less alone. Maybe we should get her some counselling, too, so that she can try and get outside with her dog. Take it for walks.'

'She's always refused counselling before, but maybe she will now. I really think you gave her hope today and saw her as a whole person, rather than just as someone who makes complaints.'

'That's the whole point of being a doctor. Looking at a patient holistically, rather than just as one set of symptoms that needs sorting.'

'You're a good doctor, Oliver.'

He appreciated her compliment. 'You are too. The way you kept her mind off the needle whilst she was having the blood test and holding her hand. A lot of doctors worried about complaints wouldn't have made any physical contact at all.'

'Like you say…she's a person. I've never been to her home before. Never seen how she lived since the accident, because she wouldn't let anybody in, no matter how hard we tried. All she'd do was have telephone appointments. To see her living like that…it made my heart ache for her.'

He wanted to reach for Lorna's hand. To squeeze it. To let her know he'd felt the same way. 'Well, we can help her now. We've seen what she needs.'

They drove back to Clearbrook, parking in a doctor's allotted bay and entering the building. Priti was in Reception and she wanted to hear how the home visit went. When they told her, she was pleasantly surprised. 'That's great! Well done. But still, just to be on the safe side, I want you both to enter documentation of that visit onto her record, stating clearly what you each did and what was said and offered.'

'Will do.'

'And I just might know someone who can help her with the house and garden. Give me half an hour and I'll get their number to you.'

'That's great, thank you. And I'll make a referral to our talking therapy service. See if they can get someone out to her.'

'Make sure they send out two people. To protect them, as much as to protect Melanie.'

Oliver nodded and headed to the staffroom to grab his lunch. He'd brought it from home and left it in the fridge. A mixed chopped salad, topped with chunks of baked sweet potato and drizzled with tahini and sweet chilli sauce. It hit the spot nicely. Though there was more potato than salad, as he was trying to increase his carbohydrates before the marathon, as carbohydrates would break down into glucose and be stored as glycogen. The glycogen, he knew, would be the thing to give a runner energy for the race and it was important to have a good store of that, so that he didn't hit the wall mid-race. It was important to eat right for such a long race, as much as it was to train right. He was steadily increasing his calorie intake, as was Lorna.

'Last big run tonight,' she said, settling into a seat beside him.

'We're going to ache tomorrow.'

She smiled. 'But I feel confident about it. Don't you?'

'Absolutely. With you by my side? I could achieve anything. Perhaps we should climb Everest next year?' He grinned to show he was joking.

'Everest? I'm no good with heights. I think we should stay nice and close to the ground. How about an Ironman?'

He looked at her. 'You want to make this a regular thing? Every year we do something for charity?'

'Why not? It's been fun. And we've steadily raised money. Have you seen the sponsorship forms in Reception? They're nearly full!'

'People have been very generous. The people here in Clearbrook are very kind and welcoming.'

'They are.' Lorna finished her tuna and pasta

dish and set it down on the table. 'Do you feel well settled in now?'

'I do. I can see myself being here as a very old man.'

She looked at him and smiled. 'What do you see yourself doing in ten years' time?'

He thought about it. 'I don't know. Maybe thinking about retirement? About travelling a little bit.'

'Alone?'

Oliver shrugged. 'You might be fed up with me by then.'

'Never.'

She said it so seriously and he knew that she meant it. He would love to think that she would go travelling with him. He'd loved seeing the world after his break-up with Jo, but he would love to show Lorna all the fabulous places he'd found. *Share* with her all the places that were important to him. He had an image then, in his mind, of them standing at the bow of a boat as it cruised down the River Nile. She would be standing there, billowing in white linen, the sun shining down on her smiling face and him stepping up behind her, kissing her neck...

He paused at the thought. He'd been trying so damned hard to keep her in the friend zone and it had been going so well. But, dammit, if his mind didn't have other ideas! It was always suggesting stuff like this to him and it really made his present situation difficult.

Because he could imagine it so clearly. The warmth of the setting sun. The sight of the city. The way her hair would dance in the breeze. Her smile as his lips caressed that softest of skin on the slope of her neck. How good she'd smell. How he'd want to wrap his arms around her and pull her close and…

He stood up and went to make a cup of tea. They had ten minutes before afternoon clinic began and he knew patients would already be in the waiting room early.

'What about you? Where do you see yourself in ten years?' he asked, turning her question back upon her.

She shrugged. 'I don't know. Probably still working, I guess. I try not to look too hard towards the future and make plans.'

'Why not?'

'Because every time I've done that I've only ever been disappointed.'

CHAPTER EIGHT

IT WAS A PERFECT, quiet country evening as they ran on the trail about fifteen miles into their twenty-two. It was balmy, no breeze. Shards of sunlight arced to the ground through the tree canopy overhead as they ran through the woods.

Lorna still felt strong. As if she still had gas in the tank and that pleased her. Made her feel hopeful for the marathon. 'I wonder if I'd be doing as well as this if I'd still been training alone,' she said.

'Of course you would. I believe in you. You're running for someone else. You're running for that lost baby and all the other families that might lose babies. That's what's keeping you going.'

She glanced at Oliver beside her. He wore a navy running shirt, navy shorts, both with a red stripe down the sides. Sweat had dampened the hair at the temples. He looked dark and sexy and she loved how he had never let her down on a training run. Not once had he dodged one. Running for that baby, for those families affected by stillbirth, was her main motivator, but Oliver beside her was another.

'Maybe, but you've kept me going, too. Having someone to talk to and to share this experience with. Forced me up those hills when I wanted to quit. I wonder if, on my own, I might've shortened some of my practice runs.'

'You've kept me going too, and not just during running.'

She slowed slightly. 'Really?'

'Sure. Look at how you got me through that whole experience with Jo. You got me through my studies. You got me through my tests and assessments. You've helped me settle in here. You've never given up on me and so I'll never give up on you. Ever.'

Lorna smiled. 'Well, I didn't get you through the *whole* cancer battle with Jo. You had years of that after we went our separate ways.'

Oliver laughed. 'Maybe, but you were still by my side, even if you weren't there.'

She risked another glance. 'Really?'

'Really. I could hear your voice. I could see your smile. Your words of wisdom. There was this one time when she told me that I could go if I wanted. The cancer had come back, she was fighting it again and she told me that I didn't have to stay if I didn't want to. That I'd not signed up for that and she didn't want to feel like she'd trapped me with her illness.'

'Really?'

He nodded. 'But I remembered one night that you and I had been together. It was when the chemo hadn't been going great and they were having to change her treatment protocols and Jo had been upset at the setback. How I'd not known what to say to her to keep her going. That the Jo I was hearing was frightened and that all I needed to do was be there and reassure her with my presence through all our difficult times. I kept hearing your voice. Your words of encouragement. I kept thinking that we both just had to be strong enough to get through to the other side and then we'd find the happiness that we'd originally begun with.'

She remembered. She remembered saying that to him. He'd looked so lost, unable to help Jo. So frustrated. Because he'd sacrificed so much to be with Jo and yet there she had been, trying to push him away, when he'd been trying to do the right thing. And she'd so wanted, that night, to wrap him in her arms and tell him it would all be okay.

When she'd gone through her own fertility battle with Craig, she'd had no one to confide in. No one she could turn to for support. Oh, she'd had friends and colleagues and family, but they'd never been through it themselves, so she'd felt as though they didn't truly understand. Not really. And there'd been so many times when she'd thought of picking up the phone and trying to track Oliver down, but fear had always stopped her. Because she'd imagined him, back then, as being in happier times with Jo. That they'd be settled, with a family of their own and that he'd spent years watching a loved one go through a health battle. Did she really want to phone him and burden him with her own?

'You stood by her like a true gentleman. You were stoic and loyal. There were times in my past when I wanted to call *you* just to hear your reassuring voice. To make me feel better about what I was going through.'

He slowed to a stop and she slowed too, coming to stand opposite him. They were both out of breath from running *and* talking.

'I wish you had called me. It would have been great to have heard your voice. We should never have lost touch.'

'No,' she agreed. It had been the singularly biggest mistake of her life. It wouldn't have changed what had happened with Craig, but it might have been easier to get through afterwards, if she could have talked to Oliver.

'I take full responsibility. I should have called you.'

'The phone works both ways. You don't have

to take full responsibility. Besides, I…' She swallowed hard at what she was about to admit. 'I lied to myself that I was too busy to keep in touch. I didn't phone because, well, I had feelings for you back then and seeing you with Jo, knowing you were with someone else—it broke me.'

Oliver stared at her. 'It broke me, too.'

She didn't know what else to say. Was he admitting that he'd had feelings for *her*? Back then? Had they been circling one another? 'You seemed so determined to be with Jo.'

'Of course. She needed me. I couldn't walk away in her hour of need and you—you being there—it kept me sane. You kept me happy. A reason to smile every day. Being with you soothed me. Strengthened me, so that I could face each day. When we parted to go our separate ways, to jobs, I…told myself I'd call you, but every time I went to pick up the phone, I stopped myself. Because I feared where it might lead and I didn't want to hurt either of you.'

She'd had no idea that Oliver's feelings towards her had been just as strong.

What had they lost? All those years they could have been together…

'We were both stuck.'

He nodded. 'I guess.'

'We're both free now.'

'I don't want to use you, Lorna, as a way to make myself feel better. I value our friendship way too much.'

'I value our friendship, too. So much! But I can't help but think about what might have been if we'd both made very different choices.'

'So do I.'

She stared at him then. Not sure what to do.

'We should start running again. Don't want to cool down. We've still got a few miles to go.'

He was right, of course, and so they set off at a good pace.

But her mind was awhirl with thoughts. How life might look now, if she and Oliver had got together instead of Oliver with Jo, or her with Craig. Would they have had many happy years? Children? Maybe even grandchildren by now? Would they be here in Clearbrook?

She felt an ache in her heart for what might have been. For what they had lost. It felt almost like the pain of grief. A mourning for something they'd never had but had wanted.

She knew she ought to feel good that she had him now as her friend. Fear had stopped them from becoming anything else before and fear was stopping them from crossing over that line now. There were no guarantees with relationships. Being the best of friends didn't automatically guarantee happiness.

But what if it was a great base they could build on, if only they were brave enough to try?

All their long runs were done now, it was time to relax, eat right, sleep well and maybe get in a small jog of just a couple of miles two or three days before the marathon.

He felt kind of odd having told Lorna how he'd once felt about her. He wondered what she'd think if he told her how he felt about her *now*?

They spoke a lot about their pasts. They talked a lot about their present, but hardly ever spoke of the future. Last night, on the run, she'd told him she didn't think of futures because she was always disappointed, and he didn't want that for her. He wanted her to be able to have dreams and make plans. He wanted her to look ahead and aspire to brilliance and happiness. Contentment.

Peace.

'We should go out for a meal,' he said, bringing her her morning cup of tea.

'We should?'

'Absolutely! To celebrate the end of the training, to celebrate our endurance, to celebrate… us. Our friendship.'

She smiled at him. 'Where do you want to go?'

'Somewhere special. Somewhere amazing. Where we both have to dress to impress. I'll get

out my tux, you get out your heels, instead of
your trainers...'

'Sounds nice.'

'I want this week to be amazing. A nice dinner. Marathon wins for the two of us...'

'We don't know if we're going to finish. I'll
probably end up with a sprain halfway or something ridiculous. Wouldn't it be better to celebrate *after* the race?'

He pretended to think about it. 'No. It has to
be before. One last pep talk.'

'Okay. Where would we go?'

Oliver sat back in his chair and took a sip of
his tea. 'Leave it with me. I'll book somewhere
and pick you up in my car.'

'All right.' She smiled back at him. 'I'll look
forward to it.'

'That's all I want.'

Lydia Swann was Lorna's last patient of the day.
Fifty-one years old, the same as Lorna, she came
in looking a little pale and a little dishevelled.

'Take a seat, Lydia. How can I help you
today?'

'I think I'm in menopause. I'm just so...' she
shook her head as she struggled to gather the
right words to explain her situation '...done in.
Exhausted. And yet I'm sleeping really well.
Last night? I went to bed at half past eight be-

cause I felt shattered and I didn't wake until eight o'clock this morning. Twelve hours! And yet I'm *still* tired. My brain is all foggy, I can't think straight. I'm bloated and I've gone off my food.' She looked directly at Lorna, with tears in her eyes. 'My mum suffered just like this.'

'It's certainly possible. You are of the age for menopause. Have you noticed any other symptoms? Any hot flashes? Night sweats? Any problems with intercourse?'

Lydia blushed slightly. 'I do get hot sometimes and, now that you mention it…sex has been a little uncomfortable, but I put that down to my new partner being a little, well, larger than I've had before.' Lydia blushed madly now.

'And he's a new partner, you say?'

'Yes. But we've known each other for a long time, we just never got together before now. There were always other partners, you know?'

She did know.

'And are you using any lubricants to help with that?'

'Sometimes. You don't always think about it in the moment, do you? Not until after when it hurts. If I'm honest, he can be a little rough, which surprises me, because otherwise he's such a nice man. I guess you can never quite know someone until you actually do.'

Lorna smiled. 'Maybe sitting down with him

and talking to him about what you like in the bedroom might help. What your expectations are. Your turn-ons. To help him understand your needs and boundaries.'

'I know I should, but it's all so new and exciting that I don't want to spoil anything, you know?'

'I understand. Have you noticed any change with your breasts?'

'Well, that's the thing that's odd. I have. And they're bigger than they were before. I thought a lack of oestrogen from menopause would make them a little *less* full. A bit droopier, if you catch my drift?'

Lorna nodded. 'And when was your last menstrual period?'

'They've always been irregular, but I think about three months ago.'

'Is there any chance you could be pregnant?'

'At my age?' Lydia seemed surprised. 'I don't… I'm not sure. Can you fall pregnant when you're menopausal?'

'If you're in menopause, then no. Menopause means that you stop producing eggs, so it would be impossible to get pregnant. But it is still possible when you're in perimenopause, which I suspect is the stage you are in. We'll need to do a blood test to confirm.'

'I'm fifty-one, Lorna!'

'I know, but I think it's worth checking, considering your symptoms, before we start thinking about menopause or HRT, or anything like that. Have you been using protection with your new partner?'

'Yes! Except…there was this one time we didn't.'

'One time is all it takes.'

'But I have grown-up children. I have a grand-daughter!'

'Look, I don't want to worry you unnecessarily. We're just checking. Ruling things out.'

'But you really think I could be pregnant?'

'Maybe. Like I said, let's rule it out.'

'And if I am?'

'Then you come back in and talk to me again. I can give you your options and choices, but obviously, if you were to be pregnant, your pregnancy would be considered high risk.'

'Because of my age.'

'Yes.'

Lydia rolled up her sleeve. 'Then let's do this. I need to know.'

'I know this is scary, but you did say your new partner was a good man. Do you think he'd make a good father?'

'He already is. He has three boys and they all adore him.'

'Okay. So let's wait and see what the blood

test says and we'll go from there. It can take a little longer to get the results, but they're more reliable. I'll book an appointment for you in two days' time and that way, whatever the result, we can be sure to meet up again and discuss options for moving forward.'

When Lydia was gone, Lorna couldn't help but wonder what her results would be. Was this simply menopause, or could she be pregnant? The odds were very small, but not impossible.

Lorna tried to imagine how she would cope if the same thing happened to her. They were the same age. But her situation was different. Lorna knew her periods had stopped. She was in full menopause—there was no chance of getting pregnant.

She'd always yearned for a family, to have a baby, so despite all the risks of having a baby aged fifty, if she were in Lydia's position, she knew she'd go through with it. But who would be the father? Oliver?

She knew instinctively that he'd make a good father. In the same way that she'd always imagined herself as a good mother. They both had so much to give.

But it's too late for me, anyway.

She'd accepted the fact that her dreams had changed. That her time for achieving them had passed. But what if she could have a new dream?

To still dream of and aspire to a happy future? She could have that still. She just had to find a way to make it happen.

Going out for dinner with Oliver this Friday was something nice to look forward to. The marathon was something that she was excited for, even though she knew it was going to be tough. Anything worth having you had to fight for.

Should she fight for Oliver to see her as more than just a friend? Or was that being selfish? That dream to have a child could still be in his grasp if he went with someone other than her and she wanted him to achieve his dreams. That was if he wanted it. Should she ask him? Directly? Because if he said he did, would she be able to bear hearing that, knowing it would end her hopes? But if he said no…

He was worried that if it didn't work, if it went wrong, then their friendship would not be the same. It was a possibility. They worked together. People might take sides. It might make the work environment uncomfortable. Look at how it had felt when they'd had that little snafu a while back…

But we overcame it. Because we loved each other so much. Maybe we could overcome anything?

She thought about what a life with Oliver would look like. Waking up together. Having breakfast together. Being at work all day with each other. Coming home in the same car, or running in together. Cooking meals that the other liked. Sharing a bed. Day after day after day.

She felt a warm glow at the thought and then a wave of sadness. For she knew it was something she would never have, unless Oliver changed his mind. Her dreams never ever came true. And she'd grown to accept that.

When she opened her front door, Oliver presented her with a small bouquet of flowers.

'Oliver! What are these for?' Lorna gasped with delight and then held them to her nose. 'They're beautiful!'

'Beautiful flowers for a beautiful lady.'

He loved it when she blushed like that. Loved how much she was surprised by the flowers. Had her husband ever bought her flowers? Had she ever had romantic treats from him? He'd been thinking a lot lately about the guy Lorna had married and what Craig had done to her at the end. Discovering his ultimate betrayal on that devastating day when she'd learned that their last attempt at IVF had failed.

He simply could not imagine doing that to her. The man had to have been crazy not to have known what he'd had right in front of him.

'You look stunning, by the way.' Lorna was wearing a beautiful cocktail dress, in the softest, palest blue. Chiffon? Or maybe silk?

'You don't scrub up too badly yourself.'

He laughed and gave her a twirl, to show off his tux to the best effect. 'Thank you.' He held out his arm, so she could slip her hand through, and then he escorted her to his car, waiting by the kerb.

He'd had it detailed. Buffed to the highest shine, inside and out. Soft jazz played on the stereo as he drove them to their destination— Marič's, a Croatian restaurant situated in the next town over.

'Have you been there before?' she asked him.

'No. But I've heard great things about it and the online reviews are glowing. The food is out of this world, apparently.'

'I don't think I've had traditional Croatian food before.'

'Nor me. But I'm hoping to find my next great taste sensation.'

The roads were pretty quiet as they drove through villages and countryside. The restaurant had ample parking and he found a spot out back, near the river that actually fed into the brook that ran through their own village.

'Stay there.' Oliver got out and walked around

the car to open her door and held out a hand to help her alight.

'Thank you.'

'You're welcome. Ready?'

'I am. I'm really hungry, too.'

'Great.'

They walked to the front door and when they walked inside, they were greeted by a waitress who took them to their table by the window. Violin music played softly in the background as the waitress poured water for their table and took their drinks order.

They took a moment to look around. The restaurant was busy, almost full. The aromas from the food were making them salivate. 'Let's choose something. I'm starving.' They picked up the menus and considered everything. 'I like the sound of the *girice*.' That was deep fried whitebait fish with mayo.

'Mmm. Think I'll go for the—hmm, I don't know how to pronounce it—*dagnje pedoče*.'

'The mussels in garlic and lemon?'

'Mmm.'

'What were you thinking for a main?'

'I think the chicken breast with the wild mushroom sauce. It says there it's served with potatoes.'

'Sounds amazing. I'm not sure what to choose,

it all sounds so delicious. Maybe the slow-cooked beef in wine and gnocchi?'

Lorna looked at him and laughed. 'We're going to have to be rolled out of here!'

They gave their orders to the waitress and clinked their wine glasses together. 'To the big race.'

'The big race.' He sipped his drink. 'Are you nervous?'

'A little. We've been waiting for it for a long time.'

'We have, and the big day is nearly upon us.'

'I think as long as I get a decent sleep the night before, I'll feel more confident. What are you going to eat the night before?'

'A big bowl of pasta with a tomato and mushroom sauce. I'm sticking to carbs and food I'm familiar with. No point in upsetting my stomach right before the race.'

She nodded. 'That's why I'm not having anything too spicy today, either.'

They chatted about the race until their food arrived. The mussels and the whitebait looked delicious and they tucked in with gusto. 'This is amazing.'

'I can see why this place has such good reviews.'

'Talking of amazing…have you noticed what's going on between Bella and Max?'

'There's definitely something. The way they look at one another.'

Lorna laughed. 'I think they think they're hiding it quite well.'

Oliver smiled and nodded. 'But they make a great couple, don't you think?'

'I do. I hope they can work out whatever's stopping them from being together.'

'Me too. They're a good match and I can't think of any couple that deserve to be together more.'

She looked at him, thoughtfully.

She could.

CHAPTER NINE

IT WAS THE day of the marathon and Lorna had not got as much sleep as she'd wanted. She'd not slept well the last two nights. Not since that meal with Oliver. Him arriving with flowers, walking her to his car as if she were some kind of lady. Opening the door for her. Getting to the restaurant.

The restaurant itself had been gorgeous. Bijou. Candlelit. Soft violin music playing in the background. Their seats by the window, perfect. And then they'd got to talking about relationships. Bella and Max's.

She'd felt so close to happiness. So close to getting a chance at pursuing a romantic relationship with him, the way she'd always dreamed. But Oliver, as always, had been cautious. Hesitant.

Had she been pushing for something that might ruin them? And if so, what did that mean? Was she trying to sabotage her own happiness? Because for a long time after Craig, she'd told herself that she was not destined for happiness. She was not destined to be happy. But that, instead, she would live a life alone.

Maybe Oliver was right to hesitate?

When he'd pulled up in front of her cottage, she'd thanked him for the ride home and got out of the car.

'Thank you for a lovely evening,' she'd said, before walking back into the cottage and closing the door.

But things felt half finished between them. Incomplete. They should have talked more about themselves, but she'd not had the courage of her convictions to do so. Doubting herself as usual.

And so, no, she hadn't slept well. Saturday morning, she'd gone out to collect her race kit and fill in any last-minute race registration forms, before coming home again. Spending all day inside, staring at the television, but not really listening to what was being said.

It was really early. Six a.m. Oliver was meant to be picking her up at six-thirty. They were going to drive to the race together. They had looked forward to this. Trained hard for this. Could she run twenty-six miles with him by her side, feeling this way? She needed to be focused on her run. Her timing. Her nutrition. Her gels. Her hydration. Pace. Not whatever this was.

Her doorbell rang and her heart thudded.

Lorna unlocked the door and pulled it open.

Oliver stood outside in a tracksuit over his race gear. She saw his number pinned to his chest. The same number would be pinned to his shorts on the leg. Like hers. 'Good morning.'

'Morning.'

'It's good weather, at least.'

'Yeah.' It wasn't brilliantly sunny. The sky was blue, but there were plenty of white clouds and there was a cool breeze.

'Ready?'

'I guess so.'

He offered to carry her kit to the car and she watched him pack it into the back and then he opened the passenger door for her. Two days ago, he'd opened the car door for her, treated her like a lady, and he was still doing it today. He'd never let her down or treated her differently.

She smiled at him.

He closed the door as she was putting on her seat belt.

Smiling, she settled into her seat and they drove out of Clearbrook, heading for the marathon.

There were hundreds of people waiting to run, dressed in all colours. Neon orange, bright pinks, blues, greens, yellows. There were even some people in fancy-dress outfits. Oliver saw one guy dressed as a teddy bear, and another on stilts. He admired their bravery to add an extra element of difficulty onto what was already a difficult race.

He and Lorna stood a little way back from the starting line, the faster professional runners and running clubs near the front. He felt apprehensive about the race, about how they'd both do. There'd been a few niggles, some slight injuries during training sessions. He felt a lot of tension and nerves and had to keep shaking out his leg and arm muscles, as if warming them up. Glancing at her, he thought Lorna seemed just as nervous. Just as uncertain. He knew she'd struggled with her self-belief during this and he wanted her to feel as if she could do anything.

'We're going to climb mountains today.'

'As well as a marathon? I didn't sign up for that.' She laughed, nervous.

'Metaphorical mountains. We're ready. We can do this. We've trained hard.'

'I don't want to let anyone down. You. Me. Yasmin. My charity.'

'You won't.'

'How do you know?'

'Because I know you. And you're not doing this for yourself. You're doing it for others and you will kill yourself to finish this race for them and for all those families that your sponsorship money will help.'

She nodded, but he could see that she still didn't believe it. Maybe she wouldn't until she'd crossed the finishing line? He'd always considered himself a good support, a great partner, but what if he wasn't as good as he thought? Look at how much support and advice he'd given Jo. And look at how that ultimately ended.

His one main relationship in life had begun on unsteady ground and it had ended badly. That was his experience. That relationships ended badly. That he wasn't good enough. What if he wasn't enough for Lorna, either?

He didn't want to let her down and nor did he want to enter a relationship with Lorna with a clause going into it about what would happen if it ended. It felt almost fatalistic. Pessimistic. But he was just being practical. Sensible. Trying to stop the hurt before it began, just in case. Though maybe, like a marathon, you had to go through the pain to feel the joy?

He wanted the race to be a success, but he also wanted any future relationship he got involved in to be a success, because it was something he had waited for his whole life.

He reached for her hand and squeezed it. 'Ready?'

'As I'll ever be. You?'

'I'm good.' He squeezed her hand again, raised it to his lips and kissed it.

She smiled at him.

He loved the way she smiled at him. The way she blushed. That coy look she did. It was beautiful. She was beautiful. She always had been.

'Runners! The race begins in ten! Nine! Eight!'

Maybe the marathon, this long race they were about to enter, was some sort of metaphor for them. Their relationship, their friendship, had been like a marathon. Long. Sometimes difficult. Occasionally they'd hit a wall, but they'd always found strength in the other. Running by her side and keeping her safe and strong and supported and loved was just like a relationship itself.

He knew he would stay by her side.

'Seven! Six! Five!'

The crowd joined in with the countdown. On-lookers, those not running, stood behind metal barriers and clanged bells and blew whistles and cheered. Some held cardboard signs above their heads with messages of hope. Everyone here wanted everyone else to finish. To do well.

'Four! Three! Two! One! Go!' A horn blared and the runners in front of them surged forwards and he let go of Lorna's hand and began to run beside her.

They would get through this. He had no doubt in his mind at all.

They would cross the line *together*.

* * *

The first ten miles went by easily. Lorna felt strong. Powerful. As if her stamina would last for ever with Oliver at her side. But in mile eleven, there was a series of hills and the initial excitement of starting the race was over and she began to think about how many miles were left.

Another fifteen miles!

But she kept going. She kept thinking about Yasmin and the baby she'd lost to stillbirth. That was who she was running for. To raise money for a charity to help Yasmin and other families like theirs, who had lost a precious baby.

She understood their pain. Yasmin and her husband had also gone through IVF to fall pregnant with their son, Adam. He had been a most wanted child and once Yasmin had fallen pregnant after months of trying, she had sailed through her pregnancy as if she had been born to do it. Like all prospective new parents, they had begun to plan for their child. Bought pushchairs and a car seat, a crib, a Moses basket. They'd spent hours deciding on names, had even sent Lorna pictures of the nursery when it had been completed. They'd hired an artist to paint a mural on the wall. The room had looked amazing. When Yasmin had gone into labour naturally, she and her husband had excitedly gone into hospital, preparing for their lives to change in the most dramatic way possible—through the joy that was new life.

Yasmin had been monitored through some of her contractions and the midwives had noticed one or two decelerations of the baby's heartbeat. They'd turned up her synthetic oxytocin, a drug used to increase strength and rhythm of contractions. She'd bounced on a ball. She'd walked and paced around her bed. She'd sucked on gas and air, but her cervix hadn't been dilating as well as it ought to. Baby Adam's heart had kept slowing and it had become an emergency and Yasmin had been rushed into surgery for an emergency caesarean, where she'd been put to sleep. She'd not wanted that, but had been willing to forgo the moments after birth holding her child, if it had meant they would both survive.

By the time the surgeons had opened her up, Adam had been floppy and blue and, despite efforts to revive him, he had been born sleeping. Yasmin had woken expecting to see her baby in a cot beside her bed. Instead, she'd found her husband red-eyed and pale. In shock. And no crib beside her bed.

She'd been devastated. She'd screamed and blamed herself. She'd sunk into depression for a while, but Lorna had been there for her, as much as she'd been able, encouraging them to feel whatever they'd needed to feel to deal with their grief.

She'd sat with Yasmin for many hours and she hated the fact that this still happened to so many babies every year. Born sleeping, with no reason why. An autopsy on Adam had discovered a coarctic aorta that hadn't been picked up on scans. A narrowing of this vital main artery. His heart hadn't been strong enough to deal with the contractions and birth process. Yasmin had a reason, but so many parents did not.

It happened to far too many. Nearly two hundred families who would suddenly find themselves bereft.

Adam's death had occurred just over a year ago. Yasmin and her husband had been terrified to try again and Lorna understood that fear that conflicted with the powerful need to hold a baby in your arms. And so she was running for them and, no matter how hard this race got, no matter how steep the hills or rough the trails, she would keep going.

'You okay?' Oliver asked.

'Yeah. You?'

'I'm good. But I think we might have run the last two miles too quickly. We need to slow our pace a bit if we're going to finish strong.'

'All right.' It felt good to ease off a little. She pulled a gel from her pack and ripped it open.

The gels helped with energy levels on long runs, providing high carbohydrates and essential electrolytes to keep her fuelled. Plus, they were easy on the stomach. She passed one to him.

'Apple?'

'Of course.' She knew what his favourite flavour was. They'd practised. Tried out many different varieties and stuck to the ones they had tried and tested.

The crowds were good. Kept them going for the next few miles. Lorna recognised one or two faces, smiling and waving and cheering as she and Oliver passed.

By mile twenty, her legs ached, her feet hurt and her ankle was throbbing and she pulled up. Oliver came to a stop beside her. 'What's wrong?'

'My ankle.' She turned it this way. That. Rubbed at it. 'Something's wrong.'

'Sprained?'

'No, just…hurts. What if I can't keep going?'

'We've not got far to go! You can do this! Even if we walk over that line, you're going to finish this race!'

She was grateful for his confidence, but she wasn't feeling it. The roads seemed endless and her thoughts had been on Yasmin and baby Adam and her own lost chance at a family and here she was, yet again, putting others first and not herself by trying to push through the pain. Was it so wrong to want to feel selfish on occasion? 'You go on, without me. I'll catch up.'

'Not a chance! Here.' He grabbed her arm and draped it around his shoulder. 'I'll support you, but we're not stopping. Come on. Walk with me.'

They walked for a mile. The pain began to ease a bit and the awkwardness of being this close to him felt uncomfortable.

If he were mine, I could cry!

She had to stop again briefly to rearrange her socks that had begun to fall down. The temptation to stop and sit for a while was huge. Especially because they were near someone's house and the aroma of fried bacon was issuing from the windows and all Lorna could think of was a bacon sandwich. Instead, she took her last gel and ploughed on, with Oliver's encouragement.

By mile twenty-four, she looked at him, realising they'd never run this far together, ever, and there were only a couple of miles to go. Two more miles and then they could stop. Two more miles and she would have achieved something she had never achieved before and she would have raised a couple of thousand pounds for a charity to help families going through the worst pain ever. Her legs might hurt. Her body might hurt, but that pain was temporary. It would pass.

The pain of families that lost their precious babies would never go away.

I think I can do this!

Lorna felt a surge of adrenaline and she and Oliver began to pick up their pace. They were going to finish around the five-and-a-half-hour mark, which was amazing, because she'd thought it might be six hours or more.

Eventually, the finish line was in sight. An arch of balloons in red, white and blue and a huge crowd of cheering onlookers.

Lorna reached for Oliver's hand and grasped it as they ran towards the line, picking up their pace for a final surge of excited energy, and as they crossed, they raised their hands high and whooped and hollered and slowed to a stop, instantly being draped with a foil-like wrap by race marshals and helpers. The foil wrap helped them keep warm as their body temperatures dropped once the race was done and then someone was there draping a medal around each of their necks.

'We did it!' she gasped.

'We did it!'

She fell into his arms. Clung to him. Kissed his cheek and never wanted to let go. But race marshals moved them on and slowly they made their way to the recovery area.

* * *

Oliver had driven her home and when they'd got to her cottage, she'd invited him in to celebrate their triumphant completion of the marathon. They'd drunk some wine, ordered pizza, and eaten it whilst watching some romcom on television. Now they sat beside each other on the sofa, tired and aching.

'What a day.' They both still wore their medals. The pizza-delivery guy had looked confused when he'd seen them hanging around their necks. But now Lorna held hers up in front of her. 'First medal I've ever won.'

'I think I got a medal once before. Winning a rounders competition against a neighbouring school. Wasn't as posh as this, though.'

'I'm thinking of getting one of those box frames, putting in my running top, my number and this medal so I can put it out on display. Maybe at work?'

'Good idea.' He reached for her hand. 'But I have a better idea.'

'What's that?' she asked as he turned to face her on the couch.

Oliver reached up to stroke her cheek and she smiled. She felt content. Happy. Tired. But not too tired for Oliver to be touching her. To be showing her affection. Love. She was pleasantly surprised, but she wouldn't question it.

'Are you happy?'

She nodded. 'I am. Are you?'

He looked thoughtful. 'Today was incredible. To achieve what we did today made me realise what a great partnership we are. What a great team we have always been.'

She smiled. 'I'm glad.'

'I know I said before that I didn't think we should be any more than friends, but twenty-six miles is a lot of thinking time and running by your side, being there with you, being a part of something amazing with you, made me realise how I always wanted that to be true.'

'We are amazing,' she said. 'Amazing friends.'

'We could be more.'

Lorna stared hard at him. Did he truly mean it? Was this their moment? 'I need you to be clear.' She thought she knew what he meant, but she didn't want to make a move and be wrong! To be rejected right now would be too much.

'I think that… I'd like to try and be more than friends.'

Lorna stared, heart pounding in a way it hadn't during the marathon!

She gazed into his eyes. She gazed at his lips. How often had she dreamed of kissing him? Or knowing him physically? Intimately? 'You mean it?'

He nodded. 'I want you.'

Lorna could hold back no longer. She leaned in and wrapped herself around him and she held him. Enjoying the feel of him in her arms. Why had he resisted for so long? Yes, he'd wanted freedom and not to feel restricted by another romantic relationship, but when had Lorna ever made him feel restricted? With her, he could be free! And able to do anything!

'You and I have had a long day. I don't want to push for something whilst you're tired.'

'I don't feel tired any more!' She sat back and looked at him, her eyes sparkling with happiness. 'I feel like I could run another marathon.'

He laughed at her joy. Loving it.

'I do need a shower, though. I'm stinky and I have mud on my legs.'

He smiled, and she could see he was picturing her in the cascading water. 'A shower sounds good.'

'Do you...want to join me?'

Oliver stood and offered her his hand. 'That sounds even better.'

Okay. She definitely liked where this was heading. Lorna took his hand and led him up the stairs. The delicious anticipation of what was ahead of her caused her heart to race, her skin to grow hot and every nerve ending to come alive. Moments ago, she'd felt herself sated and maybe she was in some ways. Her hunger was satisfied. Her conscience clear now that she had run that big race and satisfied all the people that had sponsored her and offered money to a good cause.

But sexually?

She'd not been sexually satisfied for a long time. So many nights she had spent alone in the last few years. Occasionally dating. But never tempted enough to bring anyone back or to go to theirs, so she'd learned to satisfy herself.

But it was never the same. Never the same as someone else's touch.

She walked him through her bedroom and towards the en suite. It wasn't a huge bathroom, but the shower was large enough to fit two quite nicely.

Lorna switched on the shower and then turned to face him, suddenly feeling apprehensive. Almost shy. It had been so long since she'd last undressed in front of a man and to undress in front of Oliver...

But he must have sensed her nerves for he stepped towards her and took her face in his hands and kissed her gently. 'We don't have to do anything you don't want to do.'

'That's just it. I want to do it all.' She flushed with heat, her desire for him, her need for him, pulsing through her body. She'd waited for him for so long. They'd both waited. And the sweetest, *best* things came to those who waited.

And she knew she needed to show that, because Oliver was a gentleman. He had always been a gentleman and he would never force her to do anything that she wasn't comfortable with.

Yet she was comfortable. She was excited. She just couldn't believe the time was now. That she was about to have the man she had wanted for years. That they were going to take their relationship to the next level. And so she reached for his tee shirt and lifted it slowly above his head, revealing his chest and stomach.

She was so used to seeing him in a shirt and tie. Or a tee. But he had a fine body. A perfect body, in that it wasn't ripped or overly muscular. It was just right. A broad chest, the shape of strong muscles in his arms, a stomach that wasn't washboard flat, but like hers.

He's made for me.

And then she took hold of the bottom of her own tee and raised it over her head, exposing herself in her running bra. Exposing her midriff, that she knew had got a little added extra, a little mid-life padding since menopause had hit, but that didn't matter. She was who she was and when she looked into his eyes, she saw admiration and desire.

'You're beautiful,' he whispered.

'So are you.' She laid her hands upon his chest, trailing them down over his stomach, admiring every inch. Taking in how he felt. Then she reached his shorts and saw his arousal for her. She ran her hands over him and he closed his eyes and let out a soft sigh of pleasure.

It made her feel good to see the effect her touch had on *him*. She marvelled at it. She wanted to see more. She wanted to hear him groan. Gasp. All the things. And so she slipped her hand inside his shorts and he pulled her towards him and began to kiss her.

He was hot and heavy in her hand. She could feel the heft of him, the weight. The solidity. She wanted it for herself and she let go, slipping off her own shorts and underwear and pushing herself up against him. Rubbing. Pressing. Teasing.

'Wait.' Oliver pulled off the rest of his clothes and took her hand, pulling her into the shower, gasping as the steamy water hit their bodies.

She felt his hands upon her. Exploring. Discovering. She felt as if she might explode if she didn't feel him inside her, but he turned her so her back was to him and his hands explored her breasts, her waist, her sex, as his lips caressed the side of her neck.

Lorna pressed herself back against him, opening her legs to give him better access.

It had never been like this with Craig. And if it had been, she couldn't remember it. Sex might have been fun for them once, but then conception had become all about laboratories and petri dishes and her legs up in stirrups with doctors between them, rather than her husband. It had become a clinical thing. A procedure, rather than a sexual experience.

They'd begun to abstain, because Craig had said he was frightened after each implantation to damage her or disturb the pregnancy and so he'd stayed away from her, the distance between them becoming a chasm, so that physical need had got lost in the infertility journey they had been on. She'd noticed the distance between them but had considered it normal. They had been under stress. They hadn't been trying to get pregnant the same way that other couples did. They had needed help. The act of conception had not been about two people any more, but about many— fertility specialists, doctors, nurses, lab techs, phlebotomists.

But what she was doing now was just about them. About her and Oliver and as the hot water and his hands and mouth continued to explore her, she knew she was going to one hundred per cent own it. Live every second. Devour sensation and arousal and pleasure as Oliver gave it to her. As she took it for herself. Because this was just about them.

In that moment.

Together, as they'd always been meant to be.

CHAPTER TEN

HE COULD HAVE stayed in Lorna's bed for ever. Last night had been…

Well, there are no words.

Everything he'd ever done in his life, every choice that he had made, even if he'd felt ninety-nine per cent sure of something, there had always been a voice of doubt, but not last night. Last night he had been more sure of being with Lorna than he ever had about anything and he couldn't quite believe he had made himself wait that long, until he could be sure.

But he'd *had* to be sure, because any doubt would have ruined the moment and he'd not wanted anything to ruin that.

Last night had been the most singularly beautiful night of his entire life.

They'd enjoyed a huge amount of foreplay in the shower, exploring one another's bodies, but then they'd moved into the bedroom to make love, which they had done, once, twice, three times, before he'd snuggled into her, being the big spoon, and fallen asleep with her in his arms. They both must have been so exhausted, because they were still like that when he woke.

He was used to waking early. It was Monday and they both had to be at work, but first, he wanted to do one last special thing before they had to return to work and reality hit.

So he reluctantly pulled himself from between the sheets and sneaked downstairs to make them breakfast. He wanted to give her breakfast in bed. After yesterday? They were both physically spent and then, after last night's extra-curricular exercise, they both needed to replenish some much-needed and valued calories, if they were to get through a long work day.

Her fridge was well stocked. Healthy. As he'd expected it would be. Lorna was always making sure she ate right. So he made them both pancakes and drizzled them with maple syrup and fresh berries and took up a tray, laden with coffee and fresh fruit juice, too.

Lorna was just sitting up in bed as he pushed open the bedroom door. 'Good morning!'

She smiled hesitantly and looked so beautiful, with her sleep-swollen face and mussed hair. 'Is that for me?'

'It's for us both. I hope you're hungry?'

Lorna nodded, pulling the covers up over her.

'We had quite the workout yesterday.'

She smiled as if agreeing.

'Finishing that race was amazing. Crossing the line with you? Superb. But being with you, physically, was just on another level for me.' And he meant it. It was. And he wanted this for the rest of his life.

'My legs hurt.' She reached out to massage them through the bedsheet.

He laughed. 'Anything else?' He couldn't help it. He felt as if he was on a high. Nothing could bring him down.

She shook her head. She was being very quiet. A little subdued. Maybe this was how she was in the morning?

He poured her coffee into her cup, trying not to spill it. 'I've been thinking. Thinking *a lot*. Because I want to feel this good all the time and I want us to have this for ever. Feel this way together, for ever.'

Lorna smiled and deliberately forked in a mouthful of pancake as if she couldn't respond because she was eating.

'And so I'm just going to be crazy here, Lorna, and leap in with both feet, because I think we've both waited long enough.'

'Long enough for what?' She frowned at him, unsure.

'To move in with one another. To be a real couple. Get married, eventually.'

She looked at him in shock. 'What?'

'I mean it, Lorna. I love you and I want to be with you. For ever.'

She stared back at him. 'What are you saying?'

'I love you, Lorna Hudson. I think I've always loved you, but I know now that I am *in love* with you.'

Lorna seemed to stop breathing. 'What?'

He nodded, smiling at her. 'You are beautiful. Strong. Incredible. Enduring. You've never let me down and you're always ready with a smile and a hug and I want that for ever. But not as friends. As something more. If you're ready for that, too?'

She stared at him in horror. 'You said…*married*. Are you asking me to marry you?'

He guessed he was. 'Yes.'

Lorna swallowed her pancake and looked away, as if suddenly nervous.

Her response scared him. Wasn't this what she'd wanted? She'd pushed for this. For them to have a relationship. *He'd* been the hesitant one.

'We ought to get ready for work.'

'But—'

She suddenly threw back the duvet and got up and headed into the en suite. He heard her lock the door.

It wasn't the reaction he'd expected.

Had he judged this incredibly wrong?

Cursing, he got off the bed and began to get dressed.

Lorna stood in the bathroom. Completely still. In shock. Her mind replaying his words for her over and over again.

Move in with one another. Be a real couple. Get married.

A couple of days ago he'd not wanted to move beyond friendship and today he wanted to get married?

She ought to be happy, she knew. All of yesterday, during the race, she had been strengthened with him by her side, and last night? Last night had been incredible. She'd not known it was possible to love someone like that. Be loved by someone like that and for something to feel so right!

But his words scared her. If she said yes, she was dooming him to the prospect of no children ever. Not naturally, anyway, and she couldn't imagine either of them would then want to go through a long adoptive or fostering process, or anything like that. What they'd begun last night, finally, after so long…and she could have a real chance of happiness here!

Yet he had a chance at a real family with someone else. She'd not thought he would move so fast as this. Why hadn't she asked him about children? Why didn't she know? Would she be enough for him? Just him and her?

She'd thought she'd wanted that. To be with Oliver. They'd lost so much time apart already and she did want to be with him.

But marriage scared her. She could only think about what he would be losing by choosing her. She'd been married before and it had all gone wrong. Going through a divorce had been one of the worst things to ever happen to her, but, more than that, the feeling that she just wasn't enough to have kept her husband had left her self-esteem reeling.

What if she said yes to Oliver and the same thing happened? What if he left because they couldn't have a child?

He knows my age. He knows I'm menopausal. He knows what being with me would mean. Maybe it could be okay?

She couldn't bear to not be enough for him.

To lose him again.

Oh, why did I push for this? For a relationship? How did I think it was going to go?

'Lorna…' Oliver said her name softly. He had to be standing on the other side of the door. 'Lorna. Please come out and speak to me. We need to talk about this, before we go in to work.'

She didn't know if she was strong enough just

yet. She needed to gather her thoughts. 'You go. I'll meet you there,' she called out.

There was silence for a moment and then he said, 'I'm worried, Lorna. Are you okay?'

'I'm fine. Just please go and I'll see you later.'

'I don't want to go. We need to talk about this.'

'You've already said too much.'

'What do you mean? Please come out and talk to me. Face to face.'

But she knew that she couldn't. She couldn't face him. Not right now. She needed space, she needed time. To breathe. To compose herself so that she could react in a less emotionally distraught manner. Not right now. Not when it was all so raw. 'Please, Oliver. Please just go! I'm begging you.'

He must have heard the pain and upset in her voice, because she heard a whispered, *'All right...'* Then she heard his footsteps leave the room and head downstairs.

Softly she opened the bathroom door and listened to him moving around downstairs and then the opening and closing of her front door.

The finality of that front door closing broke her.

She gazed at the running gear on the floor and she remembered what it had been like to start the marathon with him. The way he had supported her and not left her side. The smile on his face every time he brought her tea in the morning at work, how good she felt when he sat down in the patient's chair in her room and they chatted about their day. She remembered how he'd helped Melanie, how he'd taken extra time to make sure he was doing the right thing by a patient that many had wanted to dismiss. The fun they'd had at medical school. The date at Verity's. His consistency at always being there for her.

Was she going to let him walk away?

She imagined him walking out on her for ever and never again having a night like they'd shared last night. Never being with the guy that had kept a buttercup she'd once held under his throat because he considered it special. The ache she felt in her heart made her realise that she couldn't do it. She couldn't lose him. Not this quickly. And he'd not said that they ought to get married straight away. He'd said *eventually*. Giving them both time to adjust to a second chance. A new beginning, with an old friend. An old love. A timeless and eternal love. Because she had always loved him and her reaction just now...had that hurt him? Had it made him feel rejected? She didn't want him to feel that way—she'd just been scared. And she was human. She was allowed a moment of hesitation, right?

Lorna rushed down the stairs and yanked open the front door. 'Oliver!'

He was about to pull away from her kerb when he saw her. He switched off the engine and got out of the car. 'Lorna. Are you okay?'

'I'm good. I'm fine. Look, I'm sorry, just now, for how I reacted—you scared me. Talking of moving in and marriage. All the things I'd failed at before. I got scared because I don't want to fail at them with you. Not *you*. You're my world. My everything. I couldn't bear to fail at something as big as marriage with you. I've had one big failure in life and it took me a long time to get over it.'

'I don't want to fail either.'

'But I'm not sure you've properly thought this through.' She had to be sure. She had to.

'I've thought of nothing else.'

'But…' She looked down, could feel her heart breaking at what she was doing. 'You could still have a real family with someone else. You can't do that with me. I'm in menopause, my periods have stopped, but with someone else…you could.'

She had to say it. Finally. After all this time, she had to remind him. Just in case. Because before he'd come here, she'd been ambling along through life just fine, thank you very much, and she'd been content enough. She'd never been a roller-coaster girl. She didn't need peaks of excitement and troughs of despair in her life. She needed to keep things on an even keel.

'Is that what you think I want?'

'I don't know! All I know is that I still think about what *I've* lost. What I will never have. You went through the same thing, so you know that pain. That agony. But you still could try. I can't believe I'm saying this after last night, which was wonderful and amazing and a night I will never, ever forget, but I need to tell you. Remind you. I couldn't bear it if you were to walk away from me because you realised you were trapped in a situation you hadn't fully thought through.'

'I have thought it through. Having a child was my dream once upon a time, but I've moved past that. Have I mentioned it since? Kids are wonderful, but I don't judge you or your worth on whether you can provide me with a child. I just want you to let me love you, and allow yourself to be loved in return. Can you do that?'

'Of course I can!'

'Then that's all I need.'

'Then I'm out here...' she looked down at herself, clad in only a vest top and her underwear '...wearing next to nothing because I couldn't let you leave without telling you that I love you, too.' She smiled. 'If you'll have me.'

The postman was coming up the road. Oliver

shrugged off his jacket and wrapped it around her, pulling her towards him. He let out a sigh of relief. 'You scared me for a minute there. So… you're saying that you want to? Be with me? Officially?'

'Yes. If you want to be with me too, we can do this. Day by day. Week by week and all the big things, moving in, getting engaged, married. All of it. Eventually.'

He kissed the tip of her nose. 'Then I can't wait for eventually! I love you, Lorna Hudson.'

She kissed him properly, not caring that the postman was standing there waiting to give her some letters. She laughed at the postman's expression, then turned back to Oliver. 'And I love you, too.'

EPILOGUE

OLIVER WAS MOVING IN. A lorry turned up in front of her cottage and he got out of his car and came into the house. 'Ready for your plus one?'

Lorna laughed. 'Always. I can't believe we're doing this!'

'You know, our weekends are turning out to be pretty spectacular. Last weekend we ran a marathon, this weekend I'm moving in...what's going to happen next week?'

'I don't know. Something just as good, I'm sure.'

'Let's hope.'

They spent some time directing the movers, instructing them about where the boxes should go. She and Olly had spent the week at his place deciding which furniture he would bring with him. Thankfully there wasn't too much, because when he'd rented the property it had already been partly furnished. But he had his favourite chair, a wardrobe, some bookcases and books. His guitar. His bike. His training gear. A few bits and bobs that he'd stored in the loft. His memory boxes that they'd sorted together all those weeks ago.

'Drink?'

'Love one. Oh! Whilst I think about it, I saw this.' He pulled a leaflet from his back pocket, advertising an Ironman competition next year, open to everyone, consisting of a two-point-four-mile swim, a one-hundred-and-twelve-mile bicycle ride and a marathon run at the end.

'Wow! Okay. You think this should be our event for next year?'

'Could be fun.'

She looked at him and smiled. 'I really think you and I ought to check the dictionary for the real definition of fun, because I'm not sure I remember reading about an Ironman being an example.'

He kissed the tip of her nose. 'No, but you'd look cute in bike shorts.'

She looked him up and down, pressed herself against him and stroked the front of his trousers provocatively. 'So would you.'

Oliver smiled and turned his body so that the movers couldn't see what she was doing with her hand. 'In front of strangers, Dr Hudson?'

'Want me to stop, Dr Clandon?'

'Want? No. Need? Reluctantly, yes. But hold that thought and we could pick it up again after these guys have gone.'

'Won't you want to unpack?' She continued to stroke him.

'It can wait.' He kissed her. Deeply.

She savoured every moment, still in disbelief at what was happening and how their lives were changing. There was so much to tell everyone! They'd tried to keep it secret until Oliver had moved in, but everyone at work had already guessed, so…maybe they weren't as discreet as they'd thought they were. But there was still family to tell and, though they had no doubts that everyone would be thrilled for them, they wanted the move done before telling everyone else. They wanted to keep their little bubble for as long as they could.

Lorna let him go with a sigh. 'Tea, then?'

'Great.' Oliver adjusted his trousers with a smile and went to direct a mover who was trying to bring in the wardrobe.

She gazed at Oliver. At this man who had made her the happiest woman on the planet. Good things came to those who waited, but had the world really needed to make them wait this long?

Perhaps so. They'd both still needed to grow before they could be together. To work out any last remaining baggage they had each been carrying.

Oliver was worth the wait.

This amount of happiness had been worth the wait.

And she knew she would spend the rest of her days being in love and smiling because of this man. Her soulmate.

Her guy.

As the removal guy trotted upstairs with a large box, Oliver turned to her, holding another. He smiled and passed it to her. 'I think you need to unpack this one.'

She raised an eyebrow. 'What's in it?'

'Open it and see.'

Smiling she took it into the kitchen, slicing open the tape with a knife, only to find another box inside. 'What is this?'

'So many questions.' He laughed.

She sliced open the next box. And then the next. And the next, until finally she sliced open the tape on a small box that revealed a small, velvet-lined box, wrapped in tissue paper. 'Oliver?'

'Just open it.'

Her hands were trembling. She thought she knew what it might be, but she didn't want to leap to any conclusions. Making assumptions had almost made her lose him and she didn't want to make those same mistakes. Not with him.

So she delicately unpeeled the tissue paper and slid out the blue velvet box. It had a gold catch, which she flicked open with her finger and, taking a deep breath, she pushed open the lid.

As she did so, Oliver went down on one knee. 'Lorna…you have made me complete and I love you more than I ever thought it was possible. Will you do me the honour of becoming my wife?'

Lorna gasped at the diamond solitaire ring that sat nestled within the dark blue velvet. Almost stopped breathing as Oliver took the ring from the box and held it to her finger.

He looked up at her, his gaze filled with love.

'Yes! Yes, I will marry you!'

Oliver slid the ring onto her finger and then he was standing and pulling her into his arms for a celebratory kiss.

'This is your version of eventually?' She laughed.

'I waited a week. How much longer did you think I could wait?'

She laughed and kissed him, knowing that they had the rest of their lives to be together. And it would all be absolutely perfect.

* * * * *

Look out for the next story in the
Cotswold Docs duet
Finding a Family Next Door

And, if you enjoyed this story,
check out these other great reads from
Louisa Heaton

Resisting the Single Dad Surgeon
A Mistletoe Marriage Reunion
Finding Forever with the Firefighter

All available now!